Wicked
BEAUFORT
ALEXIA JONES HELSLEY

THE
History
PRESS

Published by The History Press
Charleston, SC 29403
www.historypress.net

Front cover, right: Wade Hampton (1818–1902), governor of South Carolina, 1876–78.
Courtesy of the Library of Congress, LC–BH832-31295.

First published 2011

Manufactured in the United States

ISBN 978.1.60949.263.2

Library of Congress Cataloging-in-Publication Data
Helsley, Alexia Jones.
Wicked Beaufort / Alexia Jones Helsley.
p. cm.
Includes bibliographical references and index.
print edition ISBN 978-1-60949-263-2
1. Crime--South Carolina--Beaufort--History--Anecdotes. 2. Corruption--South Carolina--
Beaufort--History--Anecdotes. 3. Criminals--South Carolina--Beaufort--Biography--Anecdotes.
4. Beaufort (S.C.)--History--Anecdotes. 5. Beaufort (S.C.)--Social conditions--Anecdotes. 6.
Beaufort (S.C.)--Biography--Anecdotes. 7. Crime--South Carolina--Beaufort County--History--
Anecdotes. 8. Corruption--South Carolina--Beaufort County--History--Anecdotes. 9. Beaufort
County (S.C.)--History--Anecdotes. 10. Beaufort County (S.C.)--Social conditions--Anecdotes.
I. Title.
HV6795.B42H45 2011
364.109757'99--dc22
2011012084

In memory of Evelyn Masden Jones
(1920–2011)
and
For Terry, whom I married in Beaufort.

"But let justice roll down like waters and righteousness
like an everflowing stream." Amos 5:24 (NASB)

Contents

Acknowledgements

The author acknowledges with gratitude the special support of the staff of The History Press, especially Katie Parry and Jessica Berzon. Their interest and encouragement make writing a special joy. Others whose support made this book possible are Grace Cordial, historical resources coordinator, and Charmaine Concepcion, preservation associate, of the Beaufort County Library; Beth Bilderback, visual materials archivist, of the South Caroliniana Library; Dr. Chester DePratter, South Carolina Institute of Archaeology and Anthropology; Steve Tuttle and Marion Chandler of the South Carolina Department of Archives and History; Katherine Wells; and William E. Benton. For me, no book is possible without the support of my family: Terry, Jacob, Cassandra and Johnny, and especially Keiser and Justus. Terry also created the index for this publication.

PROLOGUE
Something Wicked This Way Comes

Wicked Beaufort traces three centuries of mayhem, murder and other human frailties in Beaufort and Beaufort County, South Carolina. The Port Royal area's early history is replete with treachery, cannibalism and blood. From its early blood baths in the Escamacu and Yamassee Wars through the religious enthusiasm of the Great Awakening, Beaufort saw its fair share of death, betrayal and crime. There were heinous crimes, such as the murder of the merchant Charles Purry, and wayward souls such as the Reverend William Peaseley.

In addition, the outbreak of the War for American Independence in 1776 brought military invasion and civil strife to the Sea Islands. Partisans clashed with Loyalists. During these turbulent times, kidnapping, home invasion and ambush produced cloudy days and nights of terror. The initial contest—the Battle of Beaufort in February 1779 near Gray's Hill—was a Patriot victory. Two of the British casualties are buried in St. Helena churchyard. Yet Patriot forces withdrew from Port Royal Island and left the islands unprotected. As a consequence, General Augustine Prevost, the British commander occupying Savannah, Georgia sent raiding parties that burned the parish church of Prince William Parish at Sheldon in May 1779. In June 1779, Prevost and the British occupied the town of Beaufort, where he established a hospital for his wounded men. Prevost appreciated Beaufort's waterways for their ease of access to

Prince William's parish church, Sheldon, South Carolina. The parish church of Prince William was destroyed by the British during the American Revolution, rebuilt and again destroyed by Union troops during the Civil War. Many members of the Bull family are buried in the church cemetery. *Courtesy of the Library of Congress, Frances Benjamin Johnston, photographer, LC-J7-SC-1542.*

the interior and the region's temperate climate. Temporarily retaken by the Patriots, by the spring of 1780 the British once again controlled the Port Royal area. In December 1781, the British finally withdrew from Port Royal, leaving destruction, ill will and damaged lives in their wake.

Unfortunately, the end of the Revolution did not bring peace to the Beaufort area or to its citizens. Bands of outlaws, such as James Booth, continued to plague the outlying areas. These outlaws, some of whom were former soldiers, robbed, murdered, plundered and imperiled travel. Yet within a few years, the desperate days of the postwar world gave way to the unabashed pursuit of pleasure. The early federal years were times for the "gentlemanly" pursuits of drinking, gambling and dueling. The Second Great Awakening temporarily redirected the interests in such leisure activities for the Beaufort elite, and church membership and attendance grew. By the 1830s, politics overshadowed agriculture as a popular topic of conversation, and the Bluffton Movement and other secessionist endeavors helped put South Carolina on the road to secession and Civil War. As a result, men fought and died for the "Lost Cause."

Once again, peace did not bring peace. Rather, the postwar years were ones of political realignments, of the recently freed seeking civil and political rights and of the dispossessed elite fighting a war of insurgency. Hence, the Reconstruction years were violent times as freedmen, carpetbaggers, scalawags and the former elite fought either to develop a new order or to restore an old one. One of the casualties of these turbulent times was special constable W. Fraser Matthewes.

In 1876, Wade Hampton's "Redemption" and the return to white control of the state brought more, not less, violence as the state's murder rate rose between 1878 and 1900. In 1878, a Beaufort crime had international ramifications and engendered a tenacious chase worthy of the legendary Bulldog Drummond. In the end, the determined sheriff got his man, but not without a struggle. Early twentieth-century Beaufort faced its own challenges—agricultural depression and the boll weevil, Prohibition, income tax and bank fraud. In Beaufort, the twenties spawned two very different *causes célèbres*: Richard V. Bray and his altercation with the Internal Revenue Service in 1923 and the great Beaufort banking scandal of 1928.

These tales and others are part of the warp and weft of Beaufort's story. The picturesque, at times somnolent town of old Beaufort harbors a dark and lively history. Shadows disappear down dark alleyways, secrets hide behind locked doors and sunny days at sea end in death. *Wicked Beaufort* captures vignettes of these little-studied chapters of the Lowcountry's rich history.

CHAPTER 1

Setting the Scene—Beautiful Beaufort

Historic Beaufort, "the city by the sea," is South Carolina's second-oldest city. English settlers first arrived in South Carolina in 1670. That settlement became Charles Towne, the capital of the new colony. Forty-one years later, in 1711, surveyors laid out the town of Beaufort on the site of a 1706 fort built for defense against the Spaniards. For many years, according to historian Lawrence Rowland, Beaufort was "the southern frontier of British North America."

Given the natural advantages of Port Royal harbor and the area's intricate waterways, many saw the new town as a future maritime center. However, despite its natural advantages, growth was slow. The area's strengths were also weaknesses. For example, the harbor and waterways were difficult to defend, so for many years, Beaufort suffered greatly from Spanish and Indian raids. Historically, the area was an early magnet for international intrigue as Spain, France and England jockeyed to control this strategic locale. The blood of the innocent and the guilty stained the sandy soil of old Beaufort.

On the ground, national interests dissolved into poignant stories of men and women of different ages, nationalities and ethnicities who through circumstance found hope, betrayal, despair and death under the live oaks' canopy. These stories included natives, early settlers and Africans torn from their homes. There were thieves, mutineers, murderers, fences and fanatics.

Beaufort Bay. For much of its history, Beaufort looked to the water. Generally, houses and stores along the bay faced the water, not the street. Jacob Helsley, photographer. Courtesy of the author.

Often, justice was neither swift nor fair. For example, in 1742, the Court of General Sessions, the colony's criminal court, meeting in Charles Town convicted Peter Delmesire and John Peter Brez of knowingly receiving and selling stolen goods. The court fined both men and had them post bond guaranteeing three years of good behavior. On the other hand, a female thief faced a very different sentence. Found guilty of stealing silver spoons from several houses, the court sentenced Catherine Stuart to two days of whipping and afterward to three months "at hard Labour." That year, the grand jury also criticized Michael Moore, a St. Helena Parish constable, for gross negligence. Moore, with a warrant for murder in hand, refused to arrest Martha Westberry, who was accused of murder. When he finally tried to execute the warrant, Moore was so drunk that he lost the warrant. A judge had to issue another one before the prisoner was finally jailed.

In another case involving a Beaufort-area resident, justice was more directly administered. Joseph Butler was the perpetrator and Richard Baker the victim. On April 10, 1738, Butler, the perpetrator, received a grant for 2,250 acres in Granville County (the colonial county that stretched along the Savannah River from Beaufort to Abbeville). In 1747, Governor Glen granted Butler the guardianship of William Butler, the underage son of Thomas Butler,

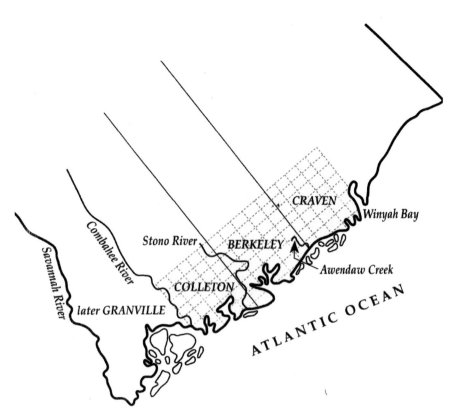

Map showing the colonial counties of South Carolina. *Courtesy of the author, Tim Belshaw, designer.*

deceased. Thomas Butler, the brother of Joseph Butler, was also a planter of Prince William Parish in Granville County. He owned land on the northwest side of the high road from the Salkehatchie River to the Pocotaligo causeway.

Richard Baker, the victim, was a planter of St. George Dorchester Parish in Berkeley County. He owned property on the Ashley River, Jack Savanna, Cow Savanna and on the Cooper River. He was a member of the Ashley River Baptist Church, founded as a branch of the Charleston Baptist Church. On November 22, 1725, Richard and his wife, Sarah Butler, donated a six-acre lot on the "public road" from Charles Town to Ashley River to the Ashley River Baptists. The donated land was part of Clear Spring or Tipseeboo Plantation.

In his will probated on December 1, 1752, Baker also left funds to support a Baptist congregation that worshiped on the northeast side of the Ashley River who, according to his will, "by Profession are Antipedo [Antipaedo]

Baptists denying Armenyanism [Arminianism] and owning the Doctrine of Original Sin Personal Election and final Perseverance." Arminianism was a school of theology that countered several core beliefs of Calvinism. In the eighteenth century, some Baptist congregations strongly supported one theological position or the other. For example, Antipaedo-Baptists denied the validity of infant baptism. The original Ashley River Baptist Church burned in 1762. Afterward in 1763, the congregation built a new brick church building on the lot that Baker had donated to the congregation in 1725. After the probate of his will, his widow, Sarah Baker of Charles Town, disposed of some of his assets and sold a sloop to William Pinckney.

On July 16, 1752, on Butler's plantation in Granville County, the two men met and tragedy ensued. The background of the incident is unknown. But Butler, holding his gun in both hands, shot Richard Baker through the left shoulder, mortally wounding him. The bullet passed through Baker and exited through his lower right back. The court valued Butler's gun at five pounds South Carolina currency and indicted Butler for felony homicide. On October 21, 1752, the South Carolina Court of General Sessions convicted Butler of manslaughter. As a result of his conviction, the court sentenced Butler to be branded on the hands, imprisoned and his property confiscated. On October 31, 1752, the "piously minded" Governor James Glen "upon the humble petition" of Butler, after the branding and imprisonment, "pardoned, remitted & released" him. Glen's pardon also suspended all property seizures.

REVOLUTION AND ITS AFTERMATH

Neither the end of the American Revolution nor independence from Great Britain guaranteed a new state of law-abiding citizens. Rather, the immediate postwar years, particularly in South Carolina, were ones of turmoil and crime. Marauding bands of escaped slaves and disgruntled whites took advantage of the disordered times to plunder and murder at will. Consequently, the 1780s were dangerous times, particularly in old Beaufort District. To meet the exigencies of the situation, the South Carolina General Assembly elected a battle-hardened partisan named Captain William Leacraft as the first sheriff for postwar Beaufort District. During the Revolution and the British occupation of Beaufort, Captain Leacraft of Hilton Head had commanded the Bloody Legion, a partisan company raised on Hilton Head Island. When Loyalist commander Philip Martinangle of Daufuskie and his troops ambushed Patriots on Hilton Head, Captain Leacraft avenged those deaths by killing Martinangle in his home with the latter's horrified wife looking on.

Unfortunately, in a number of instances, apprehending the criminal was only part of the battle. As an ad in the *South Carolina Gazette and General Advertiser* of June 10, 1783, attests, keeping the criminals in jail was also a concern. John Leacraft, sheriff of Beaufort District, originally entered the ad on May 27, 1783, seeking the capture and return of two escaped criminals. Apparently, Charles Johnston, age about twenty-two and described as stout, fair and five feet, eight inches tall, and Jacob Jones, age about nineteen and five feet, six inches in height, escaped from the Beaufort District jail on May 22, 1783. Both were dressed in various articles of homespun clothing. Sheriff Leacraft offered a reward of twenty pounds sterling for their apprehension and return. The outcome of this story is not known.

Leacraft, however, was a respected official, and in 1785 the South Carolina legislature approved additional pay for Leacraft and other sheriffs for their "extraordinary services…in making out new Juror lists and for the summoning & drawing of Jurors." Perhaps the criminals were not the only persons South Carolina courts had difficulty tracking.

By the 1790s, South Carolina was recovering economically and politically. While the threat of outlaws diminished, nonetheless, crime and fear persevered. In 1792, Sheriff Leacraft, who owned land on Skull Creek, dramatically suppressed a new threat—the Purrysburg slave conspiracy. The leading conspirators were executed and then beheaded. Leacraft then had the heads displayed on the mile markers that lined the road from Purrysburg to Coosawhatchie. According to William John Grayson, some residents of the district were offended by such barbarity and buried the heads. In 1794, the South Carolina General Assembly elected Leacraft a justice of the peace for Beaufort District.

The Murder of Richard Winn

The fear of slave uprisings was not the only concern for Beaufort residents in the 1790s. Crime and criminals were still leading topics of conversation and dread. One of these crimes was the murder of Richard Winn of Coosawhatchie Swamp in 1797. On October 28, 1797, Governor Charles Pinckney offered a reward for the capture of those responsible for Winn's death. As a result of this announcement, law enforcement captured several of the accomplices. Consequently, two days later, Pinckney issued a new

Cypress Swamp, Port Royal Island, South Carolina, 1865. Swamps and wetlands were prominent features of old Beaufort District. *Courtesy of the Library of Congress, LC-B811-3568.*

proclamation offering a reward of $400 for the apprehension of Richard Sparkman, the accused murderer.

Richard Winn lived near Cowpen Branch of the Coosawhatchie River, and Richard Sparkman may have been related to Levi Sparkman, who had fifty-eight acres surveyed on the Coosawhatchie River circa 1797. Little is known of this Richard Winn or of his accused assailant, Richard Sparkman. In 1790, according to the United States Census, the household of Richard Winn of Beaufort included three white males under sixteen, one white male over sixteen (Richard Winn), four white females and one slave. In 1800, Ann Winn, possibly the widow of Richard Winn, headed a household in Prince William Parish, Beaufort District. The census for that year lists one white male under ten, two white males between ten and fifteen, two white females between sixteen and twenty-five and one white female (Ann) over forty-five. The only Richard Sparkman listed on the 1790 census for South Carolina lived in Prince Frederick Parish, Georgetown District. His household included one white male under six, one white male over sixteen (Richard Sparkman) and three free white women. Sparkman owned no slaves. In 1800, there are no individuals named Sparkman listed as living in the state of South Carolina.

In 1807, the town of Beaufort was again in the news. Residents found the body of James Gordon "barbarously murdered" lying on a Beaufort street. As a result of this crime, the intendant (mayor) and wardens of Beaufort asked the governor for assistance. On July 23, 1807, Governor Charles Pinckney issued a proclamation offering a reward of $200. In order to collect the reward, one had to bring the miscreant to jail in South Carolina. Apprehending the criminal also required faith in the prosecution's skill and evidence as, according to the proclamation, the state would only pay the reward "upon conviction."

As the eighteenth century drew to a close, Beaufort District continued to recover, and a new cash crop—sea-island cotton—accelerated the process. By 1800, planting cotton offered new avenues to wealth for Beaufort's residents. While producing rice continued to be profitable, cotton was the new economic engine. Successful planters with their enslaved field hands prospered. As a consequence, the town of Beaufort became a popular summer resort as planters built town houses there in addition to their plantation homes.

SLAVES AND THE LAW

Success, however, came with a price. Slave property constituted much of a planter's wealth. More slaves generally equaled more wealth, and the population in antebellum Beaufort District grew increasingly African American. For example, by 1860 the population of Beaufort District was 35,894. Of that number, 29,682 were enslaved residents. The white minority employed neighborhood patrols to monitor slave activity and discipline wayward slaves. A special ad hoc court, the court of magistrates and freeholders, tried slaves accused of crimes. These courts were not sitting courts like the Court of Common Pleas and the Court of General Sessions with regular designated circuits. Rather, they only met when a crime occurred. Any magistrate could summon propertied men from the neighborhood to hear the proceedings. Generally, a session of the magistrate and freeholders court included two magistrates and three freeholders.

As the Beaufort County records were lost during the Civil War, few records of these proceedings exist. Occasionally, surviving state-level documents provide insight into how these courts functioned in Beaufort District. According to the records of the South Carolina General Assembly, on January 24, 1849 a magistrate impaneled a court of magistrates and freeholders at Washington Goethe's plantation in St. Peter's Parish, Old Beaufort District. There, the magistrate William H. Shuman (Showman) and five freeholders—William B. Ayres, Nathaniel Crapps, James E. Nix, Charles Anderson and Allen Smith—evaluated the evidence presented. All were planters in St. Peter's Parish. Two—Ayres and Crapps—were neighbors, and the other, Smith, was a neighbor of Goethe. The court found Philip, a slave belonging to Ephraim Peeples of Prince William Parish, guilty of murder and sentenced him to death. Before the sentence was executed, the court had the slave appraised. By law, the State of South Carolina compensated slave owners for slaves executed. With judgment passed and compensation set, Constable Elisha B. Wall carried out the verdict of the court and executed Philip on July 7, 1849.

The value of slaves could also tempt criminals to steal slaves for personal use or for resale. Stealing a slave or encouraging a slave to run away was a felony in South Carolina. In 1851, Seth Daniel, a Barnwell District deputy sheriff, filed an account with the South Carolina legislature for $24.44. The sum represented his expenses for transporting a prisoner to Beaufort and delivering him to the deputy sheriff of Beaufort District. The prisoner was Thomas Daley, alias Kenan, and the charge was stealing a slave. According to Daniel's account, although Daley was committed to jail in Gillisonville on July 3, 1852, he escaped on August 25, 1851. In addition, Daniel's account included fifty-three days of food for the prisoner at $0.30 per day, a fifty-four-mile round trip to deliver him to Beaufort District at $0.06 per mile and the expense of hiring a horse and buggy to transport the prisoner. In 1850, Daniel, a native of Georgia, was forty-two years old.

A SUSPICIOUS DEATH

One of the more interesting cases found from the 1850s was, in the end, a non-starter. Yet to the coroner who presided over the inquest into the death of Richard H. Simmons, the death looked anything but natural. In 1859, R.H. Simmons died unexpectedly. According to the coroner's report, the deceased was "a man of unusual good health," "muscular and active" and age "about 55 or 60 years." A neighbor reported an entertaining visit with Simmons the night before he died. Simmons lived alone with "two or three servants" and his youngest son, who was often not home. It was Simmons's living arrangements that aroused the coroner's suspicions.

According to testimony, since the death of his wife, Simmons had "kept a mulatto woman [who belonged to him]…&…had children by her." The 1850 slave schedules for Beaufort County, South Carolina, indicate that R.H. Simmons owned four slaves: a mulatto female age thirty and three mulatto children—a male age ten, a female age eight and a male age two. In 1824, Simmons of Prince William Parish, according to his tax return, owned 424 acres and five slaves. Perhaps the ten-year-old grew up and moved to Beaufort, as the 1869 militia enrollments for Beaufort County list a black

Richard Simmons age thirty living in the town of Beaufort. In 1850, R.H. Simmons, age fifty, probably already a widower, was head of a household that included Fanny, age twenty; Washington, age eleven; and John, age ten.

Prior to Simmons's death, the neighbors frequently heard the couple quarrelling. These interested neighbors pressed for an inquest, and as a result, the coroner summoned Dr. William H. Wyman and his father, Joel W. Wyman, who was also a physician, to conduct a thorough autopsy. The Wymans lived near Whippy Swamp in Prince William Parish. Dr. Wyman the father was a native of Massachusetts.

Dr. William H. Wyman tested the deceased's hair, lungs, stomach and heart. The doctor analyzed the contents of Simmons's stomach and discovered that the man's last meal had been bread or hominy. In addition, the stomach contained coal flakes and a housefly. Simmons's stomach contents may suggest a less than hygienic kitchen or the vicissitudes of antebellum living. Tests for opium, morphine and arsenic were all negative. During his examination of the deceased heart, Wyman found the cause of death: Simmons had fatty deposits in the right side of his heart. After studying the situation, Wyman reported that from his extensive tests and examinations, it was his opinion that these deposits had interfered with the flow of blood and produced "apoplexy and congestion" that killed the deceased. In other words, Simmons had suffered a heart attack and died a natural death.

The coroner's jury agreed with Dr. Wyman's findings, as Simmons "was found dead in his bed in the morning, his son sleeping in the same bed with him." The son had risen before daylight, leaving his father, as he thought, in bed asleep. The report concluded with this statement: "The young man however is quite hard of hearing!" In the final "analysis," the neighbors' suspicions cost the State of South Carolina $52.50. Wyman's bill included mileage for five miles ($2.50) plus his fees for dissection, examination and chemical analysis ($50.00).

These stories hint at the criminal past of Old Beaufort District. The full extent of arson, murder, assault and burglary in Beaufort before the Civil War is not known. Beaufort's antebellum court records were lost during the Civil War, possibly during the burning of Columbia. Yet enough pieces of the puzzle survive to paint a picture of the vagaries of the human heart and the evil that lurks within men. Such is the human condition that criminal affairs in old Beaufort ranged from the grisly, the unexplained and the incompetent to the humorous and poignant.

POSTWAR BEAUFORT

The post–Civil War years brought new opportunities for murder and mayhem to Beaufort County. The players changed and the rules were new, but the outcomes were similar. The Civil War brought federal occupation, emancipation, tax sales and threats to the long-established social order. During Reconstruction, black South Carolinians pursued civil rights and political opportunities. At the same time, some white South Carolinians worked to restore their supremacy. Pursuing these competing agendas led to voter intimidation and fraud in the 1870s. By the 1890s, Jim Crow laws and segregation ruled the landscape. Despite shifting social norms, economic exploitation, graft and corruption, man's capacity for mischief continued unabated. In that regard, new Beaufort County was little different from old Beaufort District.

A MYSTERIOUS MAN

On December 4, 1883, authorities discovered the mutilated body of a man on the railroad line near the town of Yemassee. Information on the body suggested that the deceased was F.W. Waring, a native of New York City. Railroad employees buried the unfortunate man, but how and why he met his end on the track of the Port Royal and Augusta Railroad remained a mystery.

November 1891 was a busy time in Beaufort. In the Beaufort County General Sessions Court, Judge Witherspoon considered a case involving assault and battery against defendant Francis Manigault. The grand jury submitted true bills in the following cases: murder (defendant Sam Wright), carrying a concealed weapon (defendant John Salters) and assault with intent to kill (defendant William Webb). Judge Simonton also heard arguments for a new trial in the case of T.J. Reynolds, a pension agent convicted in federal court of accepting "illicit fees."

A NEW CENTURY

By the turn of the century, Beaufort still battled its old nemesis—crime. The new century opened with a number of domestic and other disturbances. In January 1902, jealousy apparently led a boardinghouse operator to choke

Beaufort streetscape. The streets of Beaufort have a timeless quality. *Stereograph by Wilson & Havens, Savannah, Georgia, c. 1880. Courtesy of the South Caroliniana Library, University of South Carolina, Columbia, no. 12539.*

his wife. Only the timely intervention of a police constable who roomed in the house saved the woman in question. The irate husband then threatened to shoot the constable before the latter struck him. While observers agreed that only the constable's "prompt interference...saved the woman's life," both men were arrested and fined. The constable's fines were later remitted.

Later in the year, a stakeout at Captain Niels Christensen's mill brought unwelcome results. After several items of value disappeared, Fred Christensen organized a stakeout of the mill. As a result, at midnight, Christensen and an associate interrupted the night watchman, Frank Rivers, and an accomplice, Jim Brown, trying to steal valuable merchandise. Unfortunately, up until this time, the watchman had been a trusted employee. Magistrate White charged Rivers and Brown with "housebreaking and larceny, with intent to commit a felony."

Crime of a different stripe was on the docket in October 1908. The Beaufort County Court of General Sessions convicted Sam Smith, accused of larceny and burglary, of grand larceny and sentenced him to eighteen months "at such labor as he can perform on the public works of the county, or, in the State penitentiary." During the same session of court, a jury also found Edward Riley, charged with the murder of Andrew Kitchens, guilty of manslaughter and sentenced him to three years under the same conditions as Smith.

Tragedy struck in 1910. A young marine arrested for public drunkenness died when the Port Royal jail burned. A neighbor heard a cry and found the building in flames. He immediately rang the fire bell. Unfortunately, when rescuers forced open the door to the jail, flames engulfed the structure. The rescuers recovered the victim's charred remains. The young man, a native of St. Louis, Missouri, was assigned to the Port Royal naval station.

At Christmastime that year, some of Beaufort's residents eschewed "peace on earth" for skullduggery. A domestic triangle led to another death. Dan Middleton, the victim, was quietly sitting by the fire in the home of a female friend when a bullet fired through a keyhole ended his life. After an inquest, the magistrate charged the woman's estranged husband, Cornelius Thompson, with the crime.

PROHIBITION

As the century wore on, new criminal possibilities arose. Temperance societies flourished during the Progressive era, and by 1919, Prohibition was a national issue. In November 1922, Amos Bowman of Beaufort successfully defended himself against a charge of violating the Prohibition act. Yet violators were at work in Beaufort County. For example, in December 1922, federal Prohibition agents seized four thousand quart bottles of "bottled in bond whiskey" in the Cincinnati, Ohio railroad yards. James Davis had shipped 170 barrels from Seabrook, South Carolina, labeled "sweet potatoes." When opened, the barrels contained not potatoes but bottles of whiskey. Davis had shipped this special cargo to Gordon Brothers Storage Company of Chicago. Of interest, the only "James Davis" living in Beaufort County according to the 1920 census was the five-year-old son of W. Melvin Davis, a Beaufort County farmer.

Live oaks with Spanish moss, palmettos and Beaufort bay—quintessential Beaufort. *Courtesy of Jacob Helsley.*

BLUE LAWS

By May 1927, the focus of law enforcement had shifted. Sheriff J.E. McTeer announced that he planned to enforce the Sunday blue laws. Under such laws, there would be no sales of soft drinks or other merchandise or of gasoline and automobile supplies on the Sabbath. Emergency sales of gasoline or automobile supplies required the approval of law enforcement personnel. In public announcements, the sheriff encouraged motorists to fill their tanks on Saturdays and all residents to make necessary purchases between Monday and Saturday.

The 1920s, however, brought more challenges than a crackdown on Sunday sales of Coca-Cola. For Beaufort, the 1920s were a decade of unwelcome discovery, tarnished honor and civic rebellion.

Modern Beaufort is a charming southern city. Nestled in the curve of the Beaufort River, its stately homes survey broad expanses of water and salt marsh. Moss-draped mighty live oaks shade the shoreline. Sun-dappled lawns and bird songs suggest a timeless place—a reflective place—a place where present and past are one. "Wicked" seems a strange adjective for such a place. Yet Beaufort—the town, the district, the county—is a place where events and men conspire, where menace stalks and fear walks, where death and honor intertwine and where a good man can be hard to find.

CHAPTER 2
"Written in Blood"

The early history of the Port Royal (Beaufort) area is written in the blood of Native Americans, French sailors, Spanish soldiers and farmers, English planters, imported slaves and the ill-fated Scots of Stuart Town. French and Spanish adventurers were the first Europeans to visit the Beaufort area. Both found its waterways impressive, the native inhabitants generally friendly and surviving a challenge. Following Christopher Columbus's first voyage to Hispaniola in 1492, the Spaniards conquered the islands of the Caribbean, Mexico, Meso-America and portions of South America.

With the conquest of the Aztecs and Incas, great wealth flowed from the New World to the Old. Heavily laden Spanish galleons faced treacherous currents, shoals, sudden storms and pirates to bring their cargoes of gold and silver to Spain. The route of these galleons, often traveling in convoys, followed the Gulf Stream along the coast of Florida until westward-flowing trade winds guided their way homeward. Generally, the ships would encounter these westerly winds between Jacksonville, Florida, and Wilmington, North Carolina. With Port Royal harbor roughly the mid-point, whoever controlled Port Royal was a threat to the Spanish fleet. Recognizing the area's strategic importance, beginning in the 1550s Spain attempted unsuccessfully to develop a port there.

Marsh and the Beaufort River. *Jacob Helsley, photographer. Courtesy of the author.*

CHARLESFORT

Spain's rival, France, however, succeeded. In February 1562, Admiral Gaspar Coligny, a leading French Huguenot, dispatched Captain Jean Ribaut to establish a French outpost in the New World. Coligny was interested not only in furthering the imperial goals of France but also in creating a haven for Huguenots, French Protestants. As France was a Catholic country, the Huguenots periodically faced persecution, death and exile.

Born in Dieppe, Ribaut (1520–1565) was a French naval officer. On February 18, 1562, Ribaut, Rene de Laudonniere, his lieutenant, and about 150 men sailed from Le Havre, France. On May 24, they encountered the entrance to a beautiful river that they named Port Royal. In time, the name "Port Royal" applied not only to the sound but also to the largest island in Beaufort County and to the region.

Claiming the area for the king of France (Charles IX), Ribaut and his men erected a column bearing the royal arms on a nearby island. Landing on Parris Island, Ribaut and his men quickly built a sturdy bastion in the wilderness—Charlesfort. Enthusiastic about the area, Ribaut wrote glowingly of the area's valuable timber and rich wildlife (including partridges, turkey, deer and bears) and also lauded the natural advantages of the harbor he had named Port Royal. In poetic terms, he described spring in Beaufort—palmettos surrounded by trees laden with flowers and fruit and a "very good smell."

Above: View of the French exploration of Port Royal. Ribaut wrote glowingly of the Port Royal area. *Courtesy of the Library of Congress, Theodore de Bry, engraver, Jacques Le Moyne de Morgues, LC-USZ62-52514.*

Below: Chief Athore and Rene Laudonniere with column bearing the arms of France erected by Captain Jean Ribaut during the second French expedition to Florida. Ribaut had erected a similar column during his attempt to settle Charlesfort on Parris Island, South Carolina, in 1562. *Courtesy of the Library of Congress, Theodore de Bry, engraver, LC-USZ62-374.*

Despite such auspicious beginnings, this early attempt at a permanent European home in the Sea Islands also ended in failure. In June 1562, Ribaut sailed for France to secure additional supplies. He left Albert de Pierria in charge and urged him to govern wisely the men who remained in the fort. Similarly, Ribaut enjoined the men of Charlesfort to respect Pierria as if he were Ribaut. Unfortunately, Pierria was not Ribaut.

In a sense, his departure doomed the little settlement. Politics and war delayed his return, and the twenty-eight men who had voluntarily remained in Charlesfort faced increasingly difficult challenges. Expecting Ribaut's return, the men did not plant crops but instead relied upon the neighboring Indians for food. Winter arrived, but no supply ship appeared on the horizon. By January, the Frenchmen's supplies were gone, and the local Native Americans, with their food supplies seriously depleted, could offer little assistance. Then, unexpectedly, the men obtained two canoes of beans and corn, and hope returned. Yet this reprieve was short-lived. Disaster struck when fire destroyed the storehouse holding the food and also burned part of the fort. By this time, hunger and low morale were constant companions for the lonely Frenchmen. Captain Albert de la Pierria, commander of Charlesfort, did not govern wisely. Instead, he alienated the men with capricious and arbitrary punishments. For example, he hanged one aged veteran for a minor infraction and then exiled the well-liked La Chere to a nearby island with no provisions. His despotic actions exacerbated tensions and eventually sparked mutiny. The mutineers killed Pierria and chose a new captain. The new leader rescued La Chere and tried to develop a plan for survival. But by that time, even new leadership could not save Charlesfort.

Finally, in desperation, the men of Charlesfort, with the assistance of the neighboring Indians, built a crude sloop caulked with mud and Spanish moss. In April, with homemade sails, the brave little band set out for France. Encountering the doldrums of the mid-Atlantic, the men in their leaking ship quickly exhausted their meager food and water supply. Drinking salt water, eating shoe leather and facing slow and agonizing death, the starving men turned to cannibalism. They drew lots to select the communal sacrifice. The victim, so the story goes, was La Chere—the popular soldier whose banishment without food or water had sparked the mutiny. His death, however, was not completely in vain, as an English ship eventually rescued the survivors. In time, some of them returned to France, but rumors of their desperate days at sea followed them.

The fate of the French from Charlesfort was only the first of many dark chapters in Beaufort's history. The fate of the daring Jean Ribaut was equally

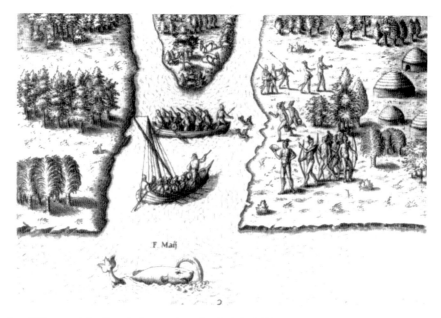

Jean Ribaut and the French fleet explore the St. John's River in Florida. *Theodore de Bry, engraver after watercolor by Jacques le Moyne. Courtesy of the Library of Congress, LC-USZ62-60966.*

dark and disturbing. Lulled by promises of food and water for his men, the shipwrecked Ribaut surrendered to the Spaniards. The Spaniards then systematically massacred all the non-Catholics, including Ribaut. The blood of Ribaut and his men stained the Florida shore north of St. Augustine.

SANTA ELENA

Spain, angry about the French incursion into land they claimed, destroyed the remnants of the French settlement on Parris Island. They seized the column Ribaut had erected claiming the land for the king of France and launched a new and this time successful effort to settle the Port Royal area. In 1566, the Spaniards under Pedro Menendez de Aviles, the governor of Florida, returned to Parris Island and built a town—Santa Elena—and a fort—Fort San Felipe—for protection. Archaeological excavations suggest that Fort San Felipe was an earthen fort with parapets and a moat. The town grew, and Santa Elena, the capital of the Spanish province of La Florida, was the most important Spanish city in North America. Its location represented the high-water mark of Spanish settlement in the interior of eastern North America.

Pedro Menendes de Aviles. This Spanish admiral founded both St. Augustine and Santa Elena. *Courtesy of the Library of Congress, Francisco de Paula Marti, engraver, LC-USZ62-102263.*

By 1572, almost fifty men, women and children lived in Santa Elena. The little town had a tailor, mercantile shops, a church and a tavern. Many of the settlers planted crops and raised livestock. Yet life was hard, and the ground produced few crops. Consequently, early in 1576 a few disillusioned settlers petitioned for permission to return to Spain. But another settler writing in 1577 painted a different picture of life in Santa Elena. He found the site fruitful and claimed to have planted orange and fig trees, grapes, wheat, barley, onions and other vegetables.

The outbreak of the Escamacu War later in 1576 ended this first chapter of Santa Elena's history. Oristo, Guale and other coastal tribes rose in rebellion. This uprising began with a sunrise attack in an Escamacu village. On a mission to secure food, twenty Spanish soldiers from Fort San Felipe were ambushed and killed. Fortunately for the settlers at Santa Elena, one escaped to spread the alarm. According to Stanley South, the Indians beheaded the soldiers and carried their heads as trophies to the Guale chiefs. Learning of the attack and deaths, the settlers at Santa Elena left their homes and fled to Fort San Felipe for protection.

The fort commander then sent out a foraging party with war dogs. Guale warriors killed the dogs and all but one of the foraging group before besieging the fort. For several hours, five hundred Indians showered the fort with flaming arrows. Fewer than twenty soldiers survived to defend the fort. Though greatly outnumbered, the commander of Fort Felipe had sufficient food and water to withstand a siege. Consequently, he was determined to hold the fort with his remaining soldiers and a few civilians. The bereaved widows of Santa Elena, however, had another idea. In a "petticoat" rebellion,

Dr. Chester DePratter and Kalla DePratter working near the golf course clubhouse, Parris Island, in the vicinity of the Spanish pottery kiln. Parris Island was the site of the Spanish settlement of Santa Elena, the northernmost Spanish outpost in eastern North America. Archaeological excavations continue to uncover pieces of Beaufort's Spanish history. *Courtesy of the South Carolina Institute of Archaeology and Anthropology.*

they forced the commander to abandon his position and transport the Santa Elena survivors to St. Augustine and Havana. From their ship, the former residents could see pillars of smoke as the natives destroyed the fort and set fire to their homes at Santa Elena. In a short time, the Spanish settlement at Santa Elena was smoldering rubble. The French had tried in 1562 and the Spaniards in 1566, and both efforts ended in failure. Weather, food shortages and failed Native American relations doomed these early attempts.

Unwilling to give up, in June 1577, the Spaniards returned to Parris Island. They erected a new fort, Fort San Marcos, and rebuilt the town of Santa Elena. Although no longer the provincial capital, the Spanish government encouraged settlers to move to Santa Elena, and for a time, the little town flourished. Settlers planted grain, vegetables and vineyards and raised cattle. They established businesses and pursued trading opportunities. For a few years, it appeared that this Santa Elena, though heavily subsidized by the Spanish Crown, might survive.

This time, however, Spanish colonial policy, not food shortages or Indian wars, doomed the town. In the summer of 1587, the little Spanish outpost became a footnote in history. The Spanish government ordered the forced evacuation of the settlers and the destruction of the settlement. Spanish officials feared English colonizing efforts at Roanoke and the raids of the English "sea dogs" (privateers) on Spanish shipping and St. Augustine. With a "circle the wagons" mentality, the leaders wanted to concentrate their limited North American resources in St. Augustine. Although the Spaniards voluntarily abandoned Port Royal, they would continue to be a threat to the region and to South Carolina's survival for decades to come.

CHARLES TOWNE, STUART TOWN AND BEAUFORT

In 1670, the English came to Carolina and settled Charles Towne. The new settlers built homes, engaged in the Indian trade, cultivated crops, raised livestock and exported naval stores. Slowly, settlement moved outward from Charles Towne. Expansion generally followed the coastline and waterways. As early as 1700, the Carolinians were getting land grants, buying acreage and establishing homes in old Beaufort District. However, the earliest attempt at a formal settlement in the area was the ill-fated Stuart Town in 1684.

Henry Erskine Lord Cardross and William Dunlop were the prime organizers of the settlement at Stuart Town. They wanted Stuart Town to be a haven for persecuted Scottish Protestants. Refusing to accept a royal decree that the king was the head of the Scottish church, many Scottish Presbyterians signed a covenant stating that only Jesus Christ could be the head of the church. Consequently, Scottish Covenanters faced political difficulties, religious persecution and death in Scotland. The years 1638 to 1688 were known to many as "the killing times." As early as 1683, Lord Cardross corresponded with the Carolina Proprietors about a possible Scottish settlement in South Carolina.

Finally, in July 1684, one group of Scots, including thirty-five political and religious prisoners, set sail for the New World. The ship's commander, Captain James Gibson, cast a pall over the proceedings by kidnapping a young woman who was on board visiting the prisoners. Against her will, he forced her to remain on board the ship until she finally escaped in Charles Towne. Upon hearing her story, the governor of South Carolina ordered her release from the captain's custody. In addition to this undesirable situation, the Scots arrived to find Charles Towne in the throes of one of its perennial pestilences. As a consequence, many of the Scots became ill, and some died. Others were so discouraged that they abandoned the venture. A remnant, however, persevered and eventually reached Port Royal. These valiant few named their new settlement Stuart Town.

Old causeway near Pocotaligo. Pocotaligo was one of the Yamassee towns. After the Yamassee War, European settlers such as Hugh Bryan moved into the former "Indian lands." *John R. Todd and Francis Marion Hutson,* Old Prince William's Parish and Plantations *(Richmond: Garrett & Massie, 1935).*

Of note for later developments, in 1684 both the Scots and the Yamassee were newcomers to Port Royal. During the winter of 1684–85, the Yamassee relocated from Florida to the Carolina Lowcountry. The English welcomed the newcomers as a potential buffer between Charles Towne and the Spaniards at St. Augustine. The Yamassee, desiring to escape the Spaniards, settled in ten towns in old Beaufort District. Among these important Yamassee towns were Pocotaligo, Pocosabo, Tomatley and Altamaha. The site of Stuart Town lay near modern Beaufort. So the new Scottish and Yamassee settlements shared lands on the southern Carolina frontier.

The Scots, who enjoyed a special relationship with the Proprietors, were independent of the Charles Towne establishment. This situation produced strained relations between the leaders of Stuart Town and government officials in Charles Towne. Interested in the Indian trade, early in their tenure, they allied with the Yamassee and in 1685 accompanied Yamassee warriors on raids against tribes living in Florida under Spanish protection. In turn, the Spaniards retaliated and destroyed the settlement in August 1686. Although the surprised residents of Stuart Town escaped, Spanish raiders plundered the town for three days, killed livestock, destroyed crops, kidnapped a few unlucky souls and then burned the settlement. A subsequent hurricane further devastated the area. While a few of the surviving Scots remained in the Beaufort area, they did not rebuild Stuart Town. Only the timely arrival of the hurricane saved Charles Towne from a Spanish attack.

By 1707, the population of Port Royal was numerous enough to want a new town. Leaders organized and petitioned for a new port—the town of Beaufort. Not only was the area accessible by sea, but also, through its intricate web of creeks and rivers, planters, sailors, scouts, Indian raiders and others could penetrate deep into the interior. Early settlers raised cattle, cultivated rice and indigo and traded with the Indians. Authorized in 1711, the new town encompassed a 1706 fort and blockhouse built to defend the area against the Spaniards. While aware of the area's bloody past, hopeful men bought lots and built homes in Beaufort. Yet almost immediately the town of Beaufort encountered grave new difficulties.

YAMASSEE WAR

The greatest early challenge to the new town was the Yamassee War of 1715–16. During the winter of 1684–85 the Yamassee relocated from Florida to the Carolina Lowcountry. The peoples known as the Yamassee included several affiliated Native American groups, such as the Guale. Different factions within the Yamassee had their own chiefs. One of the better known of these leaders was the Huspa chief, leader of the Huspa faction of the Yamassee.

Years of trade abuses, enslavement and Spanish diplomacy, however, disrupted the once harmonious Yamassee-English relations. As a result, on Good Friday, April 15, 1715, at Pocotaligo, the Yamassee attacked a team sent by the commissioners of the Indian trade to investigate rumors of Yamassee unrest. Among the first casualties were John Wright and John Ruffley, Indian traders; Thomas Nairne, the Indian agent; and John Cochran and his family. Remarkably, two men survived this attack.

One of these, Seymour Burroughs (Seamor Burrows), although seriously wounded (shot through the mouth and back), escaped to warn the inhabitants of Port Royal Island. The alerted settlers boarded a ship docked at Beaufort and in a rain of arrows set sail for Charles Town. Native warriors burned the town of Beaufort, killed over one hundred settlers in the area and captured others. A few of these captives survived their ordeal and eventually were returned to South Carolina. Most did not. For example, Colonel John Bull donated communion

Entrance to Tomotley Plantation, Prince William Parish. The name derives from one of the Yamassee towns in the area. *Courtesy of the Library of Congress, Frances Benjamin Johnston, photographer, LC-J7-SC-1548.1.*

silver to St. Helena's Church in memory of his first wife, who was kidnapped by the Yamassee. Except for her shoes, no trace of the unfortunate woman was ever found. Hugh Bryan (who figures in another chapter) was another Yamassee captive. Captured by the Huspa branch of the Yamassee, Bryan barely escaped death on several occasions. In time, however, the Huspa king took him to St. Augustine and arranged his release.

During the war, the waterways of Beaufort were favorite haunts for Yamassee war canoes. The scout boats, detailed to guard the inland waterways, were the area's first line of defense. By the end of April 1715, the South Carolinians had driven the Yamassee from Pocotaligo, and a recovered Seymour Burroughs oversaw scout operations in the area. According to Larry Ivers, in August 1715, scout crews on Daufuskie Island ambushed eight Yamassee canoes, killing or capturing the Indians. The Yamassee had been raiding unattended plantations in the vicinity and were returning to Florida with their spoils. Both Nairne and Cochran, who died in the Good Friday attack, had at different times supervised the scout boats. The scouts

St. Helena Episcopal Church, Beaufort, South Carolina, side view. St. Helena is Beaufort's oldest church. Construction began in 1724. Colonel John Bull donated communion silver to St. Helena in memory of his wife, who was kidnapped during the Yemassee War. *Alexia Jones Helsley, photographer. Courtesy of the author.*

functioned as marines, fighting from their boats or on land. In August 1716, the Yamassee surprised the Port Royal scout crew, killing all but one.

In time, the colony rallied and defeated first the Yamassee and then the Creek, Catawba and other allied Indian nations. With defeat, the Yamassee survivors decamped for Florida and Spanish protection. The Spaniards welcomed them, and an uneasy peace returned to the South Carolina Lowcountry. But life on the Sea Islands was altered forever. Planters and traders in the Beaufort area lost their livelihoods. They faced challenges to reestablish the disrupted Indian trade, replace missing slaves, replant crops and replenish lost livestock. The few settlers who ventured back into the

Castillo de San Marcos, St. Augustine, Florida, aerial view from the southwest. Reacting to the English settlement at Charles Town, the Spaniards in St. Augustine began constructing this masonry fort in 1672. *Courtesy of the Library of Congress, HABS FLA,55-SAUG,1-14.*

Beaufort area also found a new terror. Encouraged and armed by Spanish authorities at St. Augustine, Yamassee war canoes penetrated the Beaufort creeks and rivers and continued to raid unsuspecting plantations. Warriors killed, destroyed and seized individuals and livestock.

Ironically, during a 1719 attack on Port Royal Island, Yamassee warriors raided Burroughs's property, killed one of his children, kidnapped his wife and carried her to St. Augustine. There, the Huspa king saved her life, as he had earlier saved the life of Hugh Bryan (the focus of Chapter 3), and Burroughs rushed to St. Augustine to rescue her. Indian raids against Lowcountry settlers persisted, and as late as 1728, raiders killed the scout boat crew on Daufuskie Island (now Bloody Point) and carried the crew captain, Barnabas Gilbert, as a captive to St. Augustine. When James Sutherland, an Englishman, visited Beaufort in the 1720s, he found only "a few straggling houses" because, in his opinion, individuals were "afraid to settle...so near the Spaniards of St. Augustine who are continually encouraging the Indians to destroy them."

CHAPTER 3
"Judgment Is Mine"

On Sunday, September 9, 1739, slave violence shattered Lowcountry calm. A large, well-executed slave revolt erupted in Saint Peter's Parish in Beaufort District. Jemmy and his band of followers—some recently imported from Angola—murdered and pillaged their way southward along the King's Highway from the Stono River (twenty miles from Charlestown). They killed and decapitated the owner of Hutchinson's store and left his head on the outside steps. Traveling from plantation to plantation, the rebels, showing respect for neither age nor gender, indiscriminately slaughtered men, women and children. Near Stono Church, Lieutenant Governor William Bull of Prince William Parish and four others unexpectedly encountered the renegades. With this chance discovery, the rebellion was no longer a secret.

Bull and company barely evaded capture and sounded the alarm. The Stono rebels were trying to reach St. Augustine, where Spanish authorities had promised freedom to any Carolina slave who escaped to Florida. Spanish provocateurs visited Beaufort-area plantations to recruit runaways. Well on their way to freedom, the slaves, flushed with success, stopped to rest. At their camp, near the Edisto River, colonial militia forces discovered and attacked the slave insurgents. Many of the rebels died or were captured during the conflict. However, a few key leaders escaped, and for several years, South Carolina authorities worked to capture the remaining fugitives. Captured conspirators were tried and, if found guilty, executed or deported. The following year, in 1740, the South Carolina legislature enacted a new and harsher slave code. The new code with modifications would be in force

City Gate, St. Augustine, Florida, 1934. The Spaniards founded St. Augustine in 1565. *Courtesy of the Library of Congress, C.H. Brown, photographer, HABS FLA,55-SAUG,9-6.*

until emancipation in 1865. With a death toll of sixty-five, including forty-four African Americans, white South Carolinians pondered their futures and the significance of the Stono Rebellion, the largest slave uprising in the colonies prior to the American Revolution.

CONVERT AND PROPHET

One unexpected result of the Stono Rebellion was the radicalization of Hugh Bryan. Bryan was, like Bull, a Prince William Parish planter. Unlike Bull, the Great Awakening and, in particular, the preaching of the Reverend George Whitefield had altered Bryan's world view. The Great Awakening was a religious revival that swept through the American colonies, transforming lives, creating new churches and splintering established congregations. Stoney Creek Presbyterian Church in Prince William Parish

Churchyard of the original Stoney Creek Independent Presbyterian Church. Brothers Hugh and Jonathan Bryan and other converts of George Whitefield were instrumental in organizing the Stoney Creek meetinghouse near the Pocotaligo Road. *John A. Todd and Francis Marion Hutson,* Prince William's Parish and Plantations *(Richmond: Garrett & Massie, 1935).*

was an outgrowth of this movement. Arriving from England to Savannah in 1738, Whitefield and his preaching brought religious revival to the South Carolina Lowcountry and Georgia. One of his converts and more fervent followers was Hugh Bryan. In 1743, Bryan was one of the organizers of Stoney Creek Presbyterian Church. The new congregation built a meeting place and called the Reverend Mr. William Hutson as their pastor. Hutson was also a convert of George Whitefield.

As a result of his conversion, Bryan and his brother Jonathan shared the Gospel with their slaves. Historian Lawrence Rowland views the Bryan efforts as the beginning of the Christianization of South Carolina slaves. The Bryan brothers' evangelical mission, however, was not popular with most church or lay leaders. The slaves, nevertheless, responded excitedly to Hugh Bryan's preaching. The magnitude of the slave response and the enthusiasm of their worship services further alarmed the white population. With the Stono rebellion still fresh in planters' memories, few wanted to encourage slave meetings. In fact, according to the slave act of 1740, it was illegal for slaves to assemble in South Carolina.

Bryan was a devout man who studied scripture. As he surveyed the chaos of his time—a deadly yellow fever epidemic in 1739 (the one in 1732 had killed by some accounts 7 percent of the population, and during 1739 as many as 10 people died daily), the Stono Rebellion of 1739 and the great Charleston fire of 1740—he saw the judgment of God at work. For example, in addition to the lives lost during the Stono Rebellion, the Charleston fire of November 18, 1740, burned many blocks of the port city and destroyed the homes and property of 171 residents. Emboldened by his apocalyptic world view, Hugh Bryan penned a journal, revised his prophetic word and sent a copy of the final version to the speaker of the Commons House of Assembly. Although no copy of Bryan's journal is known to exist today, reports circulated that he had prophesied an apocalyptic slave uprising that would destroy Charles Town.

Peter Timothy, editor of the *South Carolina Gazette*, published Bryan's letter calling for repentance and covered the resulting furor. In his letter dated November 20, 1740, published in the March 17, 1742 issue of the *South Carolina Gazette*, Bryan cited the devastation of the great fire and asked, "Is there Evil befallen to a city and the Lord hath not done it?" Referencing past calamities, such as drought, diseases of "Man and Beast," the slave insurrection and the failed attack on St. Augustine in 1740, Bryan prayed that his fellow Carolinians, including churchmen, would humble themselves and repent of their sins, abandon "worldly goods and Pleasures" and passions and share the Gospel with their lost slaves. Colonial officials were not amused.

The *Gazette* of March 27, 1742, also carried the presentment of the South Carolina grand jury dated March 17, 1742, which excoriated Hugh Bryan for his "sundry enthusiastic Prophecies of the Destruction of Charles-Town, and Deliverance of the Negroes from their Servitude." Stephen Bull was foreman of the grand jury that wrote the presentment. The grand jury had several concerns, but only two specifically related to Bryan. First, according to the presentment, Bryan's statements were responsible for "great Bodies of Negroes" meeting together "on Pretence of religious worship, contrary to Law [the slave act of 1740], and destructive of the Peace and Safety of the Inhabitants of this Province." Slave assemblies were illegal after passage of the slave act of 1740. Consequently, members of the grand jury wanted the South Carolina Court of General Sessions to halt the religious assembling of slaves. Second, the grand jury accused Hugh Bryan, Jonathan Bryan, William Gilbert and Robert Ogle, four of the original organizers of Stoney Creek Presbyterian Church, of "propagating the aforesaid Notions, or assembling of Negroes, and teaching to them at private Houses without

Stoney Creek Independent Presbyterian Chapel, McPhersonville, South Carolina. In 1832, the original Stoney Creek church established this chapel for Prince William Parish families who spent their summers in the healthy environs of McPhersonville. *Courtesy of the Library of Congress, HABS SC-603-2.*

Authority for so doing." In other words, Hugh Bryan and the others, though not ordained to the ministry, were instructing the slaves in Christianity.

In addition, the Commons House of Assembly entered the fray. Following the grand jury's presentment, Bryan was arrested, charged with sedition and asked to defend his remarks before a legislative committee. In the end, Bryan apologized for his remarks, abandoned the public stage and returned to preach to the slaves on his plantation. He continued his ministry until his death. In 1752, slave evangelism spread to Georgia when Hugh's brother Jonathan relocated there.

In addition to his preaching, Bryan was a planter and militia officer. As a young man, Bryan had a frightening experience. During the Yamassee War in 1715, the branch of the Yamassee under the Huspa chief captured Bryan. One of the warriors claimed him as a slave. His "Indian mistress" gave Bryan a Bible and "a volume of bishop Beveridge's private thoughts, both of which the Indians had taken from some white family they had killed." Eventually the Indians took Bryan to St. Augustine, where in time the Huspa king arranged for his release.

At one time, Hugh Bryan operated the ferry that connected Huspa Neck with Port Royal Island. In 1741, Bryan purchased Cedar Grove Plantation from Burnaby Bull. Cedar Grove lay on the west side of Pocotaligo River across from Stony Creek. In 1744, Bryan married Mary Prioleau. During their time at Cedar Grove, Bryan built the house that stood on the plantation until it was burned by Federal troops during the Civil War. When he wrote his will in 1753, Bryan mentioned asking his creditors "for two years indulgence" after his death "for the more Easy discharge of my Debts." Bryan left a mourning ring to his brother Jonathan and the rest of his estate to his second wife, Mary. Bryan named his wife and his friend John Smith, a merchant in Beaufort, as the executors of his will. The will was dated January 2, 1753, and recorded on February 7, 1754. Following Bryan's death, his widow married the Reverend Mr. William Hutson, at that time pastor of the Independent Congregational Church in Charles Town. As a result of this marriage, the Hutson family gained control of the Cedar Grove property. Cedar Grove later was the home of young Thomas Hutson, who died tragically as a result of a duel in 1807.

Bryan, his visions, his preaching and his apocalyptic pronouncements spread mayhem throughout the colony and disconcerted many political and religious leaders. Although a man of conscience, his actions left fear and distrust in their wake.

CHAPTER 4

"Murder Most Foul"

S lavery was a fact of life in colonial South Carolina. The first settlers at Charles Towne brought slaves to the new colony. During the Proprietary years, colonists enslaved Native Americans as well as Africans. In time, though, most South Carolina slaves were of African descent. While the owners of rice and indigo plantations had large workforces, many small farmers, traders and merchants owned few slaves. By 1730, historian Lawrence Rowland reports that slaves were a majority of the population of old Beaufort District. Generally, house servants were the mainstays of colonial domestic life. They managed households, prepared meals and cared for the young. Masters depended upon and trusted their house servants. As a rule, house servants enjoyed special status and privileges. They were trusted members of the slave owner's "family." Such intimacy often brought a sense of safety and shared values. Few masters viewed as threats the men who drove their carriages, laid out their clothes and poured their port or the women who cooked their meals, made their beds, nursed their children and washed their clothes. Events in Beaufort, however, shattered that illusion, and after 1754, some owners may have cast more speculative eyes toward their household workers.

That year, the body of Charles Purry, a Beaufort merchant, was found brutally murdered in a creek near the town of Beaufort. Purry was the second son of Jean Pierre Purry, a Swiss agent, who founded Purrysburg, South Carolina's first township. The new township lay along the Savannah River in Granville County. As early as November 1, 1732, settlers disembarked at Charles Town for the new township. By the end of 1732, Governor Robert

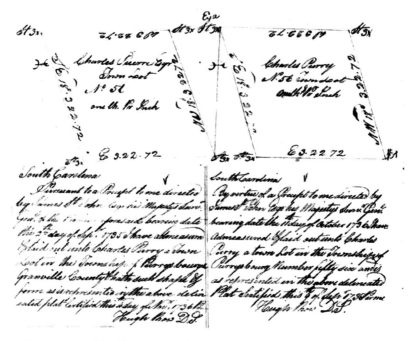

Plats of lands surveyed for Charles Purry. Purry, a Beaufort merchant, was one of the sons of Jean Pierre Purry (1675–1736) founder of Purrysburg. *Records of the South Carolina Secretary of State, Office of the Surveyor, Colonial Plats, volume 19, p. 298. Courtesy of the South Carolina Department of Archives and History.*

Johnson reported that 120 Swiss (Purry's figures suggest 152) had arrived to settle Purrysburg. In addition to land, the colony furnished these township settlers with tools, transportation and supplies. Tools included hoes and axes, and for provisions, the colony gave the new settlers corn, peas, rice, salt, beef and pork. It took three periaugers to transport the Swiss, their belongings and supplies up the Savannah River to their new home.

In its heyday, Purrysburg was home to German- and French-speaking Swiss settlers. For example, the ancestor of the prominent DeSaussure family was one of these Purrysburg emigrants. While the settlement prospered for several years, by Purry's death in 1736, it was in decline. Purry's son David returned to a prosperous career in Neufchatel, Switzerland. In the 1740s, Purry's other son, Charles, opened a store at Okatee and also transferred his primary general mercantile business to the port city of Beaufort. In early 1742, Charles Purry purchased part of Beaufort town lot no. 8. He later acquired other property in the town.

According to the St. Helena Parish register, in 1744 Charles Purry married Sarah Garvey. Subsequently, the Purrys had three children—Lucretia (b.

St. Helena Episcopal Church, Beaufort, South Carolina, rear elevation. The murdered Beaufort merchant Charles Purry was buried in the St. Helena churchyard. *Courtesy of the Library of Congress, HABS SC,7-BEAUF,1-3.*

1745), George (b. 1747) and Eleanor (b. 1751). The children were young when their father unexpectedly died. Purry's business prospered, and at his death, his estate was valued at almost £6,000. According to the recorded 1755 inventory of the Purry estate, his store carried many of the necessities and a few of the luxuries of colonial life. For example, items on hand included thread, a large selection of cloth options, padlocks, bed linen, kitchen utensils, currycombs, straw hats, buttons, pewter plates and spoons, coffee mills, axes and hatchets, hinges, shears, harpoons, scales and weights, Tunbridge & Ward powder boxes, crockery, adzes, bridles, claw hammers, pistols, mortars and pestles, turpentine, coffee, honey, mustard, rice and a bewildering array of other goods. In addition, perhaps indicative of the educational background and reading interests of Beaufort's residents, Purry's stock in trade included a wide assortment of books, including Bibles, prayer books, Virgil, Shakespeare, dictionaries, Swift, Pope, several collections of sermons (including John Tillotson, archbishop of Canterbury, and Samuel Quincy, once pastor in Savannah), the statutes of William and Mary, a Welsh dictionary, books in Latin, French and Greek, magazines, Thomas Otway's plays and, perhaps aptly, given the nature of his death, Godwin on Hell.

Among the Purry family's household goods were eight chairs, six tables, a couch, featherbeds, mattresses, blankets and sheets, tables, two tea chests, a tea kettle, silver tablespoons, trunks, looking glasses, four pairs of brass candlesticks, a chafing dish, a silver watch, a washing tub, irons and an ironing table, a frying pan, flower boxes and an old dripping pan. The inventory of the Purry estate also listed four slaves: an older married couple named Guy and Clarinda and two other women named Jenny and Silvia.

In addition, the Purry family had fresh milk, as he owned a cow, calf and heifer. The Purry household goods suggest a family of middling means, supporting the idea that he was a successful merchant. Purry also owned land in Purrysburg Township and along the Savannah River, as well as several lots in the town of Beaufort. In the end, leaving his young family to mourn their loss, Purry was buried in the churchyard of St. Helena Episcopal Church in Beaufort.

CRIME AND PUNISHMENT

On August 3, 1754, Governor James Glen issued a proclamation concerning the fifty-four-year-old Purry's murder. According to that proclamation, Purry was murdered on July 21 between the hours of nine and eleven o'clock in the evening. Apparently, the villains forced Purry to leave his home and then strangled him, stabbed him in the chest and threw his body into four feet of water. Before discarding the body, the murderer(s) attached bags holding thirty-three pounds of small shot to the body to prevent it floating. The governor enjoined all South Carolinians to find the perpetrator or perpetrators of this "barbarous and inhuman murder" and offered to pardon any accomplice who turned state's evidence.

The solution to the crime was even more horrifying to slave owners in Beaufort and throughout the province. With a slave majority, fears of slave retaliation haunted Carolina slave owners. According to the *South Carolina Gazette* of August 14, 1754, three of Purry's slaves had planned and executed his murder. One of them, Jenny—possibly the Jenny listed in the estate inventory—confessed her involvement (thus saving her life according to Governor Glen's proclamation) and implicated her brothers, Robin and Jemmy (or Jemny), as the key actors in the drama. Authorities hanged and displayed first Robin on a gibbet and later his brother. To many, the decaying corpse of an executed criminal hanging from a gibbet was a visual object lesson and served to deter other criminals from committing similar crimes.

By August 29, the paper reported that the plot instigator, with eight other conspirators, had also murdered two other white Carolinians "on the night after Mr. Purry's death." Purry's death then was but one aspect of a larger plot. From the news accounts, it appears that only the timely discovery of Purry's body prevented the slave conspirators from successfully reaching their destination—St. Augustine and freedom. However, according to entries in the

Fort Frederick, Port Royal, South Carolina. Colonial authorities built Fort Frederick, circa 1726, to protect the Beaufort area from attacks by Spanish and Yamassee raiders. *Courtesy of the Library of Congress, HABS SC-858-7.*

Commons House of Assembly, the slave conspirators may have only planned, but not executed, the other murders. Regardless, two slave conspiracies within twenty years sent shock waves through Beaufort and the surrounding areas.

The Spaniards in St. Augustine contributed to Carolina slave unrest. They welcomed South Carolina slave fugitives. Former slaves who converted to Catholicism and agreed to serve in the militia and defend St. Augustine gained their freedom. Hundreds of enslaved South Carolinians took advantage of the Spanish offer. Spanish agents also visited Lowcountry plantations to recruit and encourage runaways. Such provocateurs were a factor in the great slave uprising at Stono in 1739.

By 1738, there were one hundred slave runaways in Florida. Consequently, the Spaniards established a special settlement—El Pueblo do Gracia Real de Santa Teresa de Mose. Known as Fort Mose to the English, this settlement was, like the South Carolina townships of the 1730s, St. Augustine's first line of defense in case of an overland attack. The former slaves negotiated the right to self-government with the Spaniards, and the new settlement, despite destruction in a Carolina-led raid, eventually prospered. After the Treaty of Paris that ended the French and Indian War in 1763, the Spaniards ceded control of Florida to the British. When the Spaniards left St. Augustine, they evacuated the settlers of Fort Mose to safety in Cuba. Today, the site of Fort Mose is a Florida state park.

CHAPTER 5
"Wolf in Sheep's Clothing"

In 1712, the Commons House of Assembly authorized a parish for Beaufort–St. Helena. The Reverend William Guy was the first rector. Due to the ravages of the Yamassee War, the church of St. Helena Parish was not built until 1724. The construction of the parish church was an important milestone for the struggling town.

In 1725, the Reverend Lewis Jones arrived to minister to parish communicants. Jones cared about his parish, took his responsibilities seriously and served faithfully until his death in 1746. In his will, Jones, the epitome of a dedicated clergyman, left funds to educate poor children in the parish.

Unfortunately for its residents, St. Helena Parish was not always blessed with such dedicated ministers. A major exception in the years before the American Revolution was the Reverend William Peaseley. According to the parish register, Dr. Philip Bearcraft, secretary of the Society for the Propagation of the Gospel in Foreign Parts (SPG), recommended Peaseley, a native of Ireland, to be rector of St. Helena Parish. The SPG was a missionary organization founded on June 15, 1701, to provide ministers and teachers for the British colonies, especially those in North America. The idea for the society grew out of a study commissioned by the bishop of London and conducted by Dr. Thomas Bray. As a result of the Bray study, King William III officially chartered the SPG. Ministers and teachers were in short supply in the colonies, so the SPG fulfilled a vital function in locating and recommending ministers to colonial parishes.

St. Helena Episcopal Church, Beaufort, South Carolina, west front elevation. St. Helena is the parish church of St. Helena Parish, created in 1712. The Society for the Propagation of the Gospel in Foreign Parts recommended the Reverend Mr. William Peaseley to serve as rector of St. Helena Episcopal Church. By 1751, Peaseley and his family were in Beaufort. *Courtesy of the Library of Congress, HABS SC, 7-BEAUF, 1-1.*

By April 8, 1751, Peaseley and his family were in Beaufort. Peaseley and his wife, Mary, had two children born during his years in Beaufort: Edith in 1754 and William in 1755. Within four years, however, Peaseley faced opposition among his congregants and from the St. Helena Parish vestry. In April 1755, the vestry noted in the minutes that Peaseley wanted to leave South Carolina and wrote the SPG urgently requesting another rector. Peaseley also apparently wrote the society, citing ill health as his reason for wanting to relocate. Unfortunately, this talk of ill health and voluntary relocation was a smoke screen to hide the deep divisions that existed between the congregation and their rector. In several ways, Peaseley's conduct in office offended and disturbed his parishioners. Consequently, with congregational spirituality and unity at stake, the vestry wanted him removed and a new rector assigned.

As the months passed and they received no reply to their request to the SPG, the parish vestry, gravely disgusted by Peaseley's conduct, took unilateral action and in 1756 removed Peaseley from office. The minutes of April 19, 1756 (Easter Sunday), record that the vestry asked the public treasury to pay Peaseley the sum of £275, his six-month salary through March 25, 1756. At the same time, the vestry and church wardens gave Peaseley notice that his salary would end on September 29, 1756, and "advised him to make Provision for himself by that time." In a letter to the rector, the vestry stated that their actions were dictated by "the General discontent of your parishioners arising from the unhappy Differences which has so long subsisted and still increases." Consequently, the vestry decided to act to restore "our usual and much desired Tranquility." They also planned to seek assistance from clergy in Charles Town but pointedly reassured Peaseley that they would not reveal particular and personal details of their grievances that might be "injurious to you and your Family." They also asked Peaseley not to participate in church life but to actively seek other employment. Clearly, the members of the vestry were losing patience with Peaseley and with an unresponsive SPG.

ALEXANDER GARDEN

A few months later, on June 24, 1756, the vestry wrote the Reverend Mr. Alexander Garden Sr., who had been rector of St. Philip Church in Charles Town and commissary under the bishop of London. Garden was a well-respected Lowcountry churchman. In their letter to Garden, the vestry alluded to the "notorious" differences between the congregation of St. Helena and its rector. According to the vestry, parishioners did not attend worship services nor take communion because "they cannot receive the Sacrament from a man whose Life & Conversation prove him to have so little or no Regard for Religion or the Reputation of that sacred Order which he is a member of." The writers told Garden that they had proof of Peaseley's disgusting conduct and had tried to effect a peaceful separation, under the guise of ill health, but the SPG had not responded to their request. They then asked for Garden's assistance in locating a proper minister for their church. They also cited their deep concern for Peaseley's family. Despite the rector's failings, the vestry did not want to leave Peaseley's family without income or exacerbate their suffering.

On July 16, 1756, Garden answered the vestry's letter. He chided them for attempting to compromise with Peaseley and suggested that they immediately discharge him, draw up a list of particular charges with collaborative support and send that information to the SPG. From Garden's perspective, the vestry's concern for Peaseley and his family was secondary "when Religion and the Church of God" were suffering. Garden's primary concern was the parish and its parishioners. The personal havoc wrought by Peaseley on his own family was of secondary importance. In addition to this direct advice, Garden offered to forward their complaints when he received them to the SPG and the bishop of London with a cover letter of his own. The next move was up to the vestry.

Heeding Garden's advice, the vestry again wrote Peaseley on August 2, 1756. They rejected his counterproposals for extensions and housing allowances and reiterated their determination to end his salary on the date previously stated. In addition, they warned that rather than have him officiating at St. Helena, the vestry would order "the Church Doors…to be shut against you." They also apprised Peaseley of their intentions, if he did not vacate the position, to communicate their documented sworn allegations to the SPG and the bishop of London.

On August 21, 1756, a less than conciliatory Peaseley answered suggesting that the vestry had violated their word and shared irresponsible complaints with Garden. As a result, he feared Garden would "think me guilty of the most culpable actions, and consequently prove of the very worst Consequence to me and my Family." Peaseley went on to inform the vestry that he was traveling to Charles Town and would be happy to carry a letter for the vestry to Garden if the vestry would add specific details about their difficulties with Peaseley. For example, Peaseley suggested they could list such "indiscretions and imprudencies" as "uneasiness in my Family, my warmth of Temper in resenting injuries and such like." Specifically, Peaseley did not want the vestry to recount to Garden "the Scandelous Story" told by Mrs. Cattell's servant. As appears from other entries, the alleged story probably concerned the relationship of Peaseley and Mrs. Cattell. In other words, Peaseley asked the vestry to suggest more minor concerns, such as the rector's temper and the lack of harmony in his home, rather than the more serious allegation of sexual immorality, perhaps the source of the lack of harmony in the Peaseley home. Not only did Peaseley boldly attempt to dictate what the vestry should write to Garden, but he also urgently requested their help with a personal debt.

In a postscript, Peaseley pressed his case for debt relief. He stated that his financial situation was so dire that he had been forced to sell some of his books and asked the vestry to authorize half a year's salary. He concluded his plea with a suggestion that payment might facilitate his relocation and pleaded the deep distress of his family due to his pecuniary difficulties.

The vestry's response of August 24, 1756, reminded Peaseley of their directive of the previous April and refused to write Garden the ameliorating letter he requested. Concerning the allegation of Mrs. Cattell's (perhaps Margaret Cattell, who purchased Beaufort town lot number 304 in 1747–48) servant, the vestry tersely noted: "We wish it were the only bad one laid to your Charge." The vestry, however, did agree to authorize the rector's salary for the current term.

AN IMPASSE

In September 1756, with matters at an impasse, Peaseley traveled to Charles Town. There he discussed the situation with several colleagues. As a result of that visit, on October 7, 1756, he again wrote the vestry. This time, upon recommendation of his friends, he refused to leave his position. He alleged that without direct authorization from the SPG, he would be violating his agreement—a course of action that could adversely affect his future employment opportunities. He also stated that he had not had enough time to secure another position. Instead, he asked the vestry for an extension to allow him to serve as the church's rector with pay until Easter 1757.

The following day, a surprised vestry tersely replied to Peaseley's request. They refused his offer to serve with pay through the following Easter and seemed to wonder if concern for the opinion of the SPG or the welfare of his family were the rector's main reasons for wanting to remain in Beaufort. Peaseley was clearly a man in a serious muddle.

Next Peaseley presented his case to various clergymen assembled in Charles Town for the session of court. By this time, the Reverend Garden had died and there was no one in Charles Town familiar with the vestry's concerns. According to a letter written by the Reverend Mr. Richard Clarke, rector of St. Philip Church, to the vestry on October 20, 1756, the assembled clergy found Peaseley's account convincing and wondered if

Ships in the harbor, Beaufort, South Carolina. Beaufort's waterways were avenues for commerce and travel between the islands and with larger port cities such as Charleston and Savannah. *Courtesy of Jacob Helsley.*

the situation were as serious as had been suggested. However, as they had only heard his side, they asked the vestry to send them the particulars of their dissatisfaction with Peaseley. With the situation as it stood, the clergy in attendance could not provide the good reference that Peaseley needed to obtain another position.

The Vestry's Reply

Thus goaded, on November 5, 1756, the vestry reluctantly responded at length. After reiterating their reluctance, the vestry stated that a letter was not long enough for the full explication of their concerns and proofs. So, omitting "feuds" between Peaseley and the majority of his parish, the vestry focused on the critical elements and began with the rector's "too frequent and ill timed Visits to a Woman" who formerly lived in Beaufort. A member of the public observing Peaseley's actions had filed with Beaufort magistrate Captain Fendin an affidavit alleging immoral behavior. Another resident also reported to Fendin that he had observed "indecent familiarities" between Peaseley and the woman in question. Fendin took the matter to Peaseley and recommended that he take action to clear his reputation. When Peaseley did not respond to his suggestions nor act on the allegation, Fendin again contacted the rector urging him to address the complaint.

At that point, Peaseley met with the vestry and, rather than addressing the issue, instead complained about Fendin's treatment of him. In the end, the rector assured the vestry that he would not again visit the woman. Despite this promise, according to the vestry, he visited her "that very afternoon." Even when the vestry remonstrated with Peaseley, he continued seeing the woman. The attraction was too great. At that same time, anonymous flyers about the alleged affair appeared in public. Posted around Beaufort, the flyers disconcerted and upset Mrs. Peaseley, the congregation, the vestry—in sum, everyone but the man involved: the rector. As a result of the strained relations in the Peaseley family and the rector's "obstinate indiscretion," his disillusioned parishioners avoided church and refused to take communion, an unusual occurrence in St. Helena Parish.

Not only did Peaseley not end the relationship, but he was seen weeping in public with the woman before he left for Charles Town. And after leaving his home for Charles Town, he spent "two days and two nights" at her home, which was only four miles from his home, before embarking on his journey.

When he returned late in the evening from Charles Town, rather than going home, Peaseley instead traveled extra miles to stay with the woman in question.

In addition, the vestry stated, Peaseley, on two occasions, refused to visit the dying even when asked, so that those poor individuals died without "spiritual Comfort." Also, there were grounds for Peaseley's concerns about his temper. According to the vestry, on one occasion, he assaulted another man and drew blood, and on several other occasions, he threatened to strike others, including a member of the vestry, "for differing with him in Opinion." In conclusion, the vestry noted that while their allegations seemed "too much like a Romance," they were regrettably "certainly true."

With such damning allegations, Peaseley had no option but to relocate. He and the church again wrote the SPG. The vestry of St. Helena requested a new minister and urged the SPG to consider the importance of their parish, and Peaseley just as urgently asked the society to find him a new place of ministry.

Without a new SPG appointment, a desperate Peaseley finally took action to remove his family from Beaufort. There were few opportunities in South Carolina, but by November 12, 1758, Peaseley was rector of St. Mark Parish. Unfortunately, St. Mark was not an ideal situation, and Peaseley repeatedly had difficulty obtaining his salary from the Commons House of Assembly. Consequently, according to Peaseley researcher Otto Lohrenz, by 1764 Peaseley and his family had moved to Virginia. There, he worked as a minister until his death. No tales followed him to Virginia, and no further indiscretions are known. Beaufort's "bad apple" found grace in the Old Dominion. Yet for a few years, temptation ruled and menaced the good order of beautiful Beaufort by the sea.

CHAPTER 6
"Live Hard, Die Young"

War is a cancer, and even peace does not always cure the patient. War can become a way of life; as Jesus said in Matthew 26:52 (NASB), "For all those who take up the sword shall perish by the sword." The American Revolution was a long, difficult and bitter struggle—the longest in American history. In South Carolina, the bitterest struggles often involved Patriots and Loyalists. In the Carolina hinterlands, battle lines were not clearly drawn. Each side sought the advantage, and often innocent civilians suffered. The warring parties burned homes, stole livestock, destroyed crops, tortured and killed alleged traitors and attacked women and children. After General Benjamin Lincoln surrendered Charles Town and the Continental army in the South to the British in 1780, Patriot forces across South Carolina followed suit and also surrendered the forts they were holding. Within weeks, the British controlled all of South Carolina. The future for independence in South Carolina looked dark.

THE BRITISH IN SOUTH CAROLINA

The victorious British forces generally offered the captured Patriots parole if they took an oath not to take up arms against the King. Many welcomed the opportunity to return to their homes and families. In addition, Lord Charles Cornwallis sent his officers on raids throughout the state. Lieutenant Colonel

Brigadier General Francis Marion. Marion, also known as the Swamp Fox, was a Revolutionary War hero. He served with both the Continental army and the South Carolina militia. *Etching by Burt (Prints Marion). Courtesy of the South Caroliniana Library, University of South Carolina, Columbia.*

Banastre Tarleton, for example, outfitted his dragoons with Beaufort District horses. Major James Wemyss burned churches and intimidated Georgetown residents. Major Patrick Ferguson tried to intimidate resistors as he recruited Tories for Loyal militia regiments. In addition, the British made other blunders. They recalled paroles and asked Carolinians to take up arms against other Carolinians. They imprisoned Patriot leaders, exiled others and confiscated their estates. Of all their mistakes, raiding the countryside had perhaps the greatest long-term significance for the future of British control of North America. It was an ill-timed raid on the home of Thomas Sumter that stirred that Patriot to action. Sumter then became the unofficial lightning rod for patriotic defiance in South Carolina. Patriot sympathizers flocked to fill his ranks.

As a result, Sumter—joined by Francis Marion of the Pee Dee, Andrew Pickens of the upper reaches of the Savannah River, William Harden of Beaufort and other partisans—launched a guerrilla war against the occupying British forces. Sumter and his troops engaged the enemy while partisans such as Francis Marion harassed British supply lines before disappearing into the swamps. Harden and his men generally operated in the Coosawhatchie area, but at times Harden and Marion cooperated in bedeviling the British. Life for the men who fought with these militia leaders was challenging and dangerous. There was excitement, fear, uncertainty, sometimes defeat and at times exhilarating victory. Death stalked the lonely roads, and allegiances faltered. Without regular supply lines or pay, many of these fighters lived off the land. Old and young, black and white fought desperately in this grass-roots campaign to wrest South Carolina from British control. Then, as now, some men so challenged may find peace too tame and usual employments unexciting. They miss the chaos, the adrenaline flow and the independence. Others grew to manhood in those disorienting times and knew no other way to live. So, with the war effort winding down and peace on the horizon, in the 1780s some of these disaffected men formed gangs of highwaymen that pillaged, plundered and murdered their fellow citizens.

JAMES BOOTH

Among these outcasts was a young man named James Booth. By the time Beaufort sheriff Daniel Stevens captured him in 1783, Booth was wanted for crimes in both South Carolina and Georgia. Allegedly, on February 19, 1783, Booth and his associates killed Dr. Orr (possibly Robert or James) while he was visiting his patients. Later, they also killed another doctor (Dr. Brown) from Virginia who was investigating Orr's death. According to some

Road through the woods, Port Royal Island, South Carolina, 1865. In the turbulent years following the American Revolution, menace stalked unwary travelers on lonely roads. *Courtesy of the Library of Congress, LC-B811-3574.*

accounts, Booth's renegades not only shot but also scalped and otherwise abused the bodies of the two doctors. The South Carolina Privy Council recommended that the state offer a reward of $450 (Mexican dollars) for the apprehension of the perpetrators and offer a pardon for anyone supplying information that led to the capture. The Reverend Mr. Archibald Simpson of Stoney Creek Presbyterian Church, who attended the public auction of Brown's horse, clothes and books, noted that the miscreants killed and robbed on public roads. Both murders had happened within six miles of his lodging. Simpson also asserted that one of the gang was in town the day of the auction.

In April 1784, Governor J. Houston of Georgia wrote Governor Benjamin Guerard of South Carolina about Booth. Benjamin Guerard (1739–1788) was a veteran of the American Revolution who had been imprisoned by the British. Of Huguenot descent, he served as governor of South Carolina from 1783 to 1785. His counterpart, John Houston (d. 1796), commanded Georgian forces against the British and served as the first mayor of Savannah. Houston stated that the chief justice of the state of Georgia had examined "the notorious offender" Booth in Augusta and ordered that he be taken to Savannah, where he had been indicted for murder. Instead, Booth had been taken to Charleston. Houston was seeking justice, as he noted that "a capital Conviction in either [state] will answer the Ends of public Justice in both." He did ask that if Booth were acquitted that he be extradited to Georgia to stand trial. Houston also wrote about Booth in June. He obviously did not want the governor of South Carolina to forget or overlook his request.

Later learning of Booth's apprehension and indictment in Beaufort, on August 22, 1784, Houston again wrote Governor Guerard on the subject of Booth. Houston informed Guerard that Booth was under indictment for murder in Georgia and that a bench warrant had been issued for his arrest. Consequently, he again asked that if Booth were acquitted at his trial in Beaufort that South Carolina convey the prisoner to Savannah, Georgia, to face charges there. The Georgia governor was particularly determined that Booth face charges in Georgia. Governor Guerard reassured him of South Carolina's intention to extradite Booth if he were not convicted in Beaufort.

Apparently, Governor Guerard had launched a targeted manhunt in order to capture Booth. On March 1, 1785, Lieutenant Colonel William Davis petitioned the South Carolina House of Representatives concerning the expenses for Booth's capture. At the request of Governor Guerard, Davis had negotiated an agreement with Captain Richard Simmons and four of his men to pursue the "notorious" James Booth. Consequently, Simmons

Left: Calendar for Beaufort District Court Session of November 1784 showing James Booth's crime and sentence. Aedanus Burke, the presiding judge, signed the document. *Records of the South Carolina General Assembly, Governors' Messages and Enclosures, 1784. Courtesy of the South Carolina Department of Archives and History.*

Right: Letter of Aedanus Burke and Thomas Heyward Jr. to Governor Benjamin Guerard, dated September 8, 1784. Judges Burke and Heyward wrote the governor about the James Booth case. Aedanus Burke served in the South Carolina House of Representatives and, although he opposed ratification of the United States Constitution, in the first Federal Congress. Thomas Heyward Jr., of St. Luke Parish, was a signer of both the Declaration of Independence and the Articles of Confederation. Burke enjoyed a long and illustrious career on the South Carolina bench. *Records of the South Carolina General Assembly, Governors' Messages and Enclosures, 1784. Courtesy of the South Carolina Department of Archives and History.*

and his men had apprehended the fugitive, and Davis wanted the general assembly to validate his agreement with Simmons by authorizing payment of Simmons's expenses. Davis asked for two dollars per day for Simmons and a dollar per day for the three men he employed to capture Booth and other offenders. On March 4, the House committee considering the petition reported that the costs were "reasonable" and should be paid. The House agreed with the committee report and sent the request to the South Carolina Senate for its approval. Davis at one time represented Prince William Parish in the South Carolina House of Representatives.

Booth was tried on November 5 in the November session of the Beaufort District Court of General Sessions. Found guilty on the charge of robbery, the court, with Judge Aedanus Burke presiding, sentenced Booth to be hanged on Wednesday, November 17, 1784. Burke, a native of Ireland, was a veteran of the American Revolution and a respected jurist. Burke also served in the South Carolina House of Representatives, and although he opposed ratification of the Constitution, Burke was elected to the first United States Congress from 1789 to 1791.

Yet, due to Booth's youth, his Revolutionary service and the suffering of his family, Judge Burke, at the behest of the court, urged the governor to consider clemency. On November 11, 1784, Burke wrote Benjamin Guerard detailing Booth's charged offenses: one indictment for felony, four indictments for robbery and one indictment for burglary. Felony was a serious crime with a sentence in excess of a year. Robbery entailed taking property or money by violence or the threat of force, and burglary was breaking and entering in order to commit a crime. The Beaufort District petit jury found Booth guilty of the charges but "recommended him to mercy on condition that he would be banished from the Continent forever."

During Booth's trial, Burke learned that Booth was twenty-one years old and a Revolutionary veteran who had never fought for or supported the British. According to testimony, Booth had served as a soldier under partisan commander Colonel William Harden. With Harden, he fought with General Francis Marion at the Battle of Parkers Ferry in Colleton County. During that engagement, on August 30, 1781, General Marion, according to the historical marker, with a force of six hundred successfully surprised British troops that included Loyalists and Hessians. Marion, of Huguenot descent, was one of South Carolina's more successful military leaders. His success at harassing British supply lines was legendary. The failure of the British to capture this elusive foe led to his nickname, "the Swamp Fox." The engagement at Parkers Ferry ended Tory harassment in the area south

Francis Marion Crossing the Peedee River. During the American Revolution, the partisan leader Francis Marion used the swamps and waterways of South Carolina to military advantage. His guerrilla tactics influenced later military training. *Engraved by C. Burt after W. Ranney (Prints Kendall os). Courtesy of the South Caroliniana Library, University of South Carolina, Columbia.*

of the Edisto River. Booth therefore probably spent his youth as a guerrilla fighter struggling to survive in Old Beaufort District.

According to Burke, Booth's father and brother, also Revolutionary soldiers, died during the war. Other accounts suggest that Booth's father died before the war, leaving him an orphan at the age of twelve. During the tumult of war, in his presence, Tories murdered his only relative, an older brother. In the waning months of the war in South Carolina, as Booth remembered, "about the year 1781 he began to lie out," and since that time, according to Burke, Booth had "been the Terror of the Southern Parts of this State by his Enormities."

On November 13, 1784, the *South Carolina Gazette and General Advertiser* reported the story. After recounting the details of his trial, his previous war service and deaths of his father and brother, the reporter, in justifying Booth's death sentence, noted that "no services or political merit will atone for the violation of the laws of this Republick." Debating whether to execute, pardon or send Booth to Georgia, Governor Guerard sought advice from the South Carolina Privy Council. Some members favored execution, while one suggested a reprieve until the House of Representatives could consider the matter of a pardon. So, in the end, the governor may have pardoned Booth and extradited him to face charges in Georgia.

From available sources, there is little evidence to identify Booth's father or brother. Several men named Booth lived in South Carolina before the outbreak of the American Revolution. One possibility is William Booth, who in 1767 was living in the Goodland Swamp area of the Edisto River, Colleton County. According to Bobby G. Moss's *Roster of South Carolina Patriots in the American Revolution*, the only identified veteran surnamed Booth who died during the Revolution was John Booth. His wife received a pension from the State of South Carolina. Also, two men named "James Booth" are listed in Moss's *Roster*, but their service details do not match Booth's account. Unfortunately, the extant records rarely reflect the service of partisan guerrillas. For example, consider the story of young Andrew Jackson and the British officer in the Waxhaws. During the American Revolution, a British officer ordered a teenage Andrew Jackson to polish his boots. When Jackson refused, the officer struck the youth with his sword. The future president carried the scars until his death. So there is no way to definitely verify or rule out the story told by James Booth. Many South Carolinians fought and died during that deadly conflict with no documents to tell their stories.

CHAPTER 7
"Boys Will Be Boys"

Beaufort at the turn of the nineteenth century was a place where men enjoyed their leisure. According to William John Grayson (1788–1863), many of the former Revolutionary veterans liked to hunt, fish, drink, talk about agriculture and debate politics. A "hospitable" group, these veterans also enjoyed swearing, off-color stories and practical jokes. Grayson's autobiography offers a personal window on life in Beaufort before the Civil War. Grayson, a Beaufort native, studied law and was admitted to the South Carolina bar. Also, he was a member of the South Carolina House of Representatives and of the South Carolina Senate. In addition, Grayson served two terms in the United States Congress. A man of letters, Grayson contributed to the *Southern Review* and wrote a sketch of the life of James L. Petigru. In addition, Grayson wrote poetry. His best-known poem, "The Hireling and the Slave," was a defense of slavery. Grayson died in Newberry during the Civil War and was buried in Magnolia Cemetery in Charleston.

As he noted in his autobiography, in the early years of the nineteenth century, the men socialized often, as they were "fond of dinners, barbecues, and hunting clubs." Such group gatherings and dinners often entailed drinking to excess, so that no one traveled home sober. In fact, in some settings, leaving a dinner sober was considered an insult. The barbecue house near the Old Beaufort College was the site of many of these manly rites. Racing and fighting were other masculine pursuits, and Sunday was a day of entertainment and leisure. Public entertainment

William John Grayson (1788–1863) was a native of Beaufort. He served in the South Carolina House of Representatives and the South Carolina Senate. His autobiography offers valuable insights into antebellum life in Beaufort. Grayson was buried in Magnolia Cemetery, Charleston. *(Prints 2000) Courtesy of the South Caroliniana Library, University of South Carolina, Columbia.*

included horse racing and cock fighting. The Fourth of July was a time of such excessive drinking that public brawls were common.

HORSE RACING

By the 1790s, horse racing was a staple of the Beaufort scene. In January 1796, racing stewards Thomas Talbird and James Stuart advertised the "Beaufort Races"—two days of racing in March. The first day featured three-mile heats open to "any Horse, Mare or Gelding," and the second day consisted of two-mile heats for South Carolina–bred colts under the age of four. In December 1803, stewards J.G. Barnwell, R.B. Screven and J. Burton advertised two days of racing in Beaufort for the following January. By 1803, the races were better organized, awarded purses and designated weights for horses of different ages. For example, when running a three-mile heat, a six-year-old horse carried 129 pounds and a three-year-old horse 92 pounds. Races were generally male-only events, although female spectators could be found at higher-end affairs.

DRINKING

Drinking was prevalent at home and in taverns. In 1793, the Beaufort District Grand Jury in its presentment complained of the number of "tippling houses" (taverns) in Beaufort. The grand jury recommended that whoever was "authorized to grant licenses be exceedingly cautious" and "limit the number as much as possible." The jury also suggested that approved taverns be "chiefly on the high roads for the accommodation of travelers." The wording of the presentment suggests that the jurors wanted to reduce or eliminate taverns in the town of Beaufort. Patriotic and other special celebrations were also times of inebriation. For example, to celebrate the Fourth of July in 1803, the citizens of Beaufort had an artillery salute, a service at St. Helena Episcopal Church and an oration by Robert Barnwell. Following Barnwell's address, the attendees "retired to their different places of entertainment." At the end of the day, there were fireworks, and the citizens drank seventeen toasts. Toast number sixteen honored Beaufort District: "Peace and prosperity to it, and may it never lose sight of its own interest." The district enjoyed periods of great prosperity in the antebellum period, but peace from murder, mayhem and menace was another matter indeed.

DUELING

As Grayson observed, in the post-Revolutionary war years, dueling was an all-too-frequent practice. The fascination with dueling permeated South Carolina society. In 1838, John Lyde Wilson, at one time governor of South Carolina, wrote *The Code of Honor; or Rules for the Government of Principals and Seconds in Duelling.* For later generations, Wilson's publication was the manual for properly conducting a duel in South Carolina.

Not a fan of the practice, Grayson characterized the duelist as "the incarnation of cool, systematic, deliberate homicide." Grayson's father, John

"Satisfaction"—image of the aftermath of a duel. Thomas Hutson and Arthur Smith were both fatally wounded during their 1807 duel in Beaufort. *Engraved by J. Halpin after W.R. Buss, for* New York Mirror *(Prints 1605 os). Courtesy of the South Caroliniana Library, University of South Carolina, Columbia.*

Grayson, following General Benjamin Lincoln's surrender of Charles Town to the British in 1780, had fought a duel with a fellow Patriot officer and killed him. So it is with a special poignancy that Grayson offered a firsthand account of a tragic affair of honor fought in 1807. The principals in this duel were Arthur Smith and Thomas Hutson, two young men of great promise.

According to the published genealogy of the Hutson family, Thomas Hutson, born September 3, 1784, was a graduate of Princeton. Before his untimely death on September 15, 1807, Hutson had a bright future. He was the second son of Thomas and Esther Maine Hutson of Cedar Grove Plantation in Beaufort District. Cedar Grove Plantation lay on the Savannah River side of Pocotaligo. The elder Thomas Hutson was an officer in the American Revolution and served as a member of South Carolina's 1788 convention that ratified the United States Constitution.

Thomas Hutson's opponent was Arthur Smith, son of Peter Smith and Mary Middleton. Mary Middleton Smith was the daughter of Henry Middleton. Peter Smith's brother James married Mariana Gough. In 1838, the sons of James and Mariana Smith legally changed their surname to Rhett. The change honored Colonel William Rhett, an illustrious ancestor who in 1718 captured the infamous gentleman pirate Stede Bonnet and delivered him to Charles Town for trial and execution.

According to Grayson, the young men belonged to different parties, possibly different political parties. In 1807, Federalists and Republicans vied for the hearts of American voters. This party difference was a factor in the tragedy. Among the toasts drunk by the Beaufort Artillery for its 1803 Independence Day celebration was one worded as following: "May those who so artfully established a supposed difference between Federalists and Republicans be convinced in the hour of danger, when our common interest requires unanimity, that a true Republican is a Federalist." By 1807, party differences had split the illustrious Pinckney family. For example, Thomas and Charles Cotesworth Pinckney were leading Federalists, but Charles Pinckney had allied with the Republican Party of Thomas Jefferson.

Heated party debates were only one factor. Honor was another. The concept of honor dictated the worldview of antebellum South Carolinians. Melding beliefs and actions, members of the southern elite responded violently to real or perceived threats. Failing to defend one's honor was a source of shame. In defense of honor, men fought and died. Dueling became, to some, a way of life. William Lowndes Yancey, for example, fought and survived several duels. As he described one affair of honor, he wrote, "The blood of the only man who has ever called me a damn liar lies unwashed upon my stick [his sword stick]." Duels did not require threats or menace. Perceived slights, unapologetic sneers or, in the case of Hutson and Smith, a simple misspoken word could trigger a duel. The young gentlemen of antebellum Beaufort understood the *code duello*. They knew the dangers, the escalating steps to confrontation, the symbols and the rituals involved. In general, they preferred death with honor to personal humiliation.

For example, in 1761, Colonel Thomas Middleton, who had married Ann Barnwell, moved to Beaufort. Middleton was an uncle of Arthur Middleton (1742–1787), one of the South Carolinians who signed the Declaration of Independence. During the Cherokee War of 1760–1761, Middleton, who commanded the South Carolina troops, had frequent and public disagreements with the British commander, Colonel James Grant. Eventually, there was an open break, and a duel ensued. Grant won the duel (perhaps Middleton fired and missed) but refused to kill his opponent. This gracious gesture humiliated Middleton, and according to Lawrence Rowland, he left Charleston "under a bit of a cloud."

Robert Barnwell Rhett's house, Beaufort, South Carolina, 1862. Robert Barnwell Rhett (1801–1882) was an early advocate of secession and a member of the United States Congress. Rhett was also a relative of Arthur Smith, who died tragically in a duel in 1807. The sons of Arthur Smith's uncle changed their surname to Rhett in 1838. *Timothy H. O'Sullivan, photographer. Courtesy of the Library of Congress, LC-B8171-0155.*

As Grayson described the Hutson-Smith affair, the conflict began at a "public entertainment." Seeking to quell a minor "disturbance," Arthur Smith intervened. Thomas Hutson casually called Smith's action "officious." A so-called "kind friend" shared Hutson's indiscreet remark with Smith. Smith then queried Hutson about the slur. Although Hutson had forgotten the incident, one of his acquaintances, perhaps another "kind friend," confirmed the truth of the statement. So, manfully, Hutson admitted the misdeed. At several points, cool-headed, objective friends could, in Grayson's opinion, have averted the tragedy.

At this juncture, politics intervened. As each followed a different party persuasion, they became their factions' "champion." Regrettably, as Grayson noted, "neither party would permit" its champion to retire. Consequently, on the afternoon of Monday, October 14, 1807, the young men met with their pistols and fired, according to the news account, almost at the same time. Both shots hit their targets, and the two young men died. Smith, who was twenty-three years of age, died Monday afternoon, and Thomas Hutson, only twenty-two years old, died Tuesday morning. Their families and friends mourned such untimely loss, but the honor of Smith and Hutson remained unscathed.

In 1812, dueling became a crime in South Carolina. By law, anyone convicted of dueling served a year in jail, paid a $2,000 fine and had to post bond to ensure his future good conduct. Also, a convicted duelist could not serve in the ministry, hold public office or practice law or medicine. If a party to the duel died, then all parties who survived could be tried for murder. Unfortunately, the cult of honor was so strong that the law was generally ignored and eventually weakened during the years leading up to the Civil War. The number of duels, however, declined during the Civil War. A kinsman of Arthur Smith, Alfred Rhett, killed another Confederate officer, Ransom Calhoun, in a duel at Fort Sumter during the war.

THE BARBECUE SHED

The location of the event that spawned the Hutson-Smith duel is not known. A few years earlier, Beaufort's greatly revered barbecue shed or house would have been a likely locale. The shed stood near the first site of Beaufort College, which was located, according to Lawrence Rowland, at the corner of Bay and Church Streets. The site of many convivial affairs, the shed, as Grayson remembered, was famous for "good cheer where the race was run, where unmeasured quantities of ham and turkey, of beef and mutton, of old Jamaica [rum] and gin and wine and punch were consumed." The shed was a retreat to eat, drink, talk and celebrate. Neither fire nor flood destroyed this favorite retreat of Beaufort men. Rather, the devastating hurricane of 1804 leveled it.

To commemorate this loss, Dr. James E.B. Finley (1758–1819), a faculty member of Beaufort College, wrote a long poem. The editor of the *Charleston Courier* published the poem, "On the Fall of the Barbacue-house at Beaufort, S.C. during the Late Tremendous Storm" in its November 1, 1804 issue. In the poem, Finley waxed classical in his allusions, referring to the shed as a "rural seat of the ancient Pan" where "the jovial Sons of Pleasure oft convene, Brushing the rubbish rust of rustic life with attic humour—sportive jest and song." The last stanza bemoaned the loss of "thy sacred Temple, Mirth, that long withstood, the wasting tooth of Time, the potent rage of jarring winds, and rains, and hail, and storm" but now "lies a sad ruin." Finley obviously had a sense of humor, but the reader is left to ponder the good times and memories lost in the great storm of 1804.

Samuel F.B. Morse, a nephew of Dr. James E.B. Finley who penned the immortal lines about Beaufort's barbecue house, spent several years painting portraits in Charleston, South Carolina. *Courtesy of the Library of Congress, Mathew B. Brady, photographer, LC-USZ62-110084.*

In time, Finley left Beaufort for opportunities in Charleston. While in Charleston, Finley was instrumental in promoting the artistic career of his nephew Samuel Finley Breese Morse. During his time in Charleston (1818–21), Morse not only painted Finley's portrait but also painted portraits of a number of other Charleston residents. Morse's painting of Finley hangs in the Indianapolis Museum of Art. Morse, the painter, is perhaps better known as Morse, the inventor of the telegraph and Morse code.

By the time of the Second Great Awakening, the Beaufort social scene had changed. Under the spell of powerful preaching, Beaufort's residents joined churches and attended church services, and some even became ministers. Social life no longer centered on drinking and gambling. Men still had the leisure to hunt and fish, but Sunday was a sacred day.

CHAPTER 8
"Wrong Place at the Wrong Time"

After the Civil War, the state of South Carolina and its citizens, black and white, faced serious challenges and adjustments. Sherman's march through the state in 1865 had left a wide swath of destruction, and the bloody battles and camp diseases had destroyed almost a generation of young South Carolinians. With the reading of the Emancipation Proclamation at Old Fort Plantation on January 1, 1863, the African Americans of Beaufort District tasted freedom before their counterparts on the mainland. Since the Battle of Port Royal in 1861, Federal troops had controlled Port Royal, Hilton Head and the other Sea Islands of old Beaufort District. As a result, the Sea Islands were magnets for slaves longing to be free. Hundreds of men, women and children fled behind the Union lines. The refugees joined the hundreds of slaves left on the Sea Island plantations when their owners fled.

The outcomes of this large population of former slaves were several. First, the first African American Union regiment mustered at Old Fort Plantation (now the site of the naval hospital). Second, the federal government and northern philanthropists combined forces to minister to the educational needs of the newly freed men. This collaboration created the so-called Port Royal Experiment. In addition, the Freedmen's Bureau worked to meet basic needs for all residents, black and white, and negotiate labor contracts for the former slaves.

Even with advanced planning and a few years of experience, the postwar years were bumpy ones for the Beaufort area. Many of the freedmen continued to live in the former slave quarters. Others relocated or purchased

Road through the woods, Hilton Head Island, South Carolina, 1865. During the Civil War, following the Battle of Port Royal, Hilton Head was the headquarters for the Department of the South. *Courtesy of the Library of Congress, LC-DIG-cwpb-03274.*

land of their own. Churches and schools were important institutions to the freedmen. When the war ended, a few planters returned to face a new world of negotiated labor and unpaid direct tax claims. The United States levied a direct tax in 1861 on all states in order to finance the war effort. South Carolina's tax was $363,570.66. Consequently, Beaufort District landowners were liable for a prorated share of the tax. Tax agents came to Beaufort in 1862 to assess the tax. As most of the Beaufort District landowners had fled inland, there were many unpaid tax assessments in Beaufort District, and thousands of acres were sold at tax auctions. Former owners redeemed some of the plantations, and the government retained others.

New men were trying to operate the old cotton plantations with new rules and a newly freed workforce. Returning owners often found freedmen less than willing to reassume the subservient labor role. Black leaders flexed political muscle in the newly designated Beaufort County (under the constitution of 1868, the former districts became counties). With a heavy black majority, African Americans held elective offices in the city and county of Beaufort. In addition, the county sent a number to serve in the South Carolina House of Representatives. Beaufort's own Robert Smalls became a United States congressman.

Despite the successes, there were disappointments. Paternalism is not always appreciated, whether it is demonstrated by a slave owner for his slave "family" or a reformer with definite ideas of how the former slaves should

Sketch of an African American church on Port Royal Island during the Civil War. After emancipation, churches and schools were important centers of African American life. *Alfred R. Waud, artist. Courtesy of the Library of Congress, LC-DIG-ppmsca-21107.*

live, work, rear their families and deport themselves socially. Tensions also persisted between the agricultural laborers and the labor superintendents. Some freedmen enjoyed their independence and consequently were loath to sign labor contracts. Others preferred to live in self-managed communities. Many wanted to manage their lives without outside interference. The postwar years, therefore, were times of transition for black and white Beaufort residents.

Stolen Mules

The postwar years were also times of crime. A fatal altercation in 1868 illustrates the difficulties of the new world order. Trying to locate and retrieve stolen property (specifically, his mules), J. Fraser Matthewes complained to magistrate John A. Porteous. In response, Porteous appointed Matthewes a "special constable" to pursue the criminals. In an agricultural world, mules were essential for cultivating crops. Their theft was a significant economic loss.

Matthewes suspected that Peter Holmes was the thief and that Holmes had taken the stolen mules to the old DeSaussure plantation (possibly on

African American settlement, Mills Plantation, Port Royal Island, South Carolina, 1862. In 1862, following the Battle of Port Royal, most white residents fled Beaufort District. Often the former slaves continued to live in the quarters on the plantation. *Timothy H. O'Sullivan, photographer. Courtesy of the Library of Congress, LC-DIG-cupb-00762.*

St. Helena Island). Consequently, on February 4, armed with a warrant, Matthewes and a posse visited the old DeSaussure plantation in search of the stolen mules. The posse included Harmon Van Ness, a relative of Matthewes, and four African Americans. The only two African Americans named were Billy Middleton and Smart Polite. Matthewes owned an adjoining plantation in the vicinity of the DeSaussure plantation.

For some time, the DeSaussure land had not been cultivated, and the residents who lived in the settlement there preyed on neighboring plantations. When Matthewes and his posse arrived at the settlement, they encountered resistance. Proceeding to the cabin of Peter Holmes, Matthewes asked admittance. Only a week before, authorities had traced stolen property to Holmes and reclaimed it. Now, confronted with another irate property owner, Holmes refused to open the door. Behind the closed door, Van Ness heard Holmes cock his gun and tried to reason with him. At that point, the matter became a community affair.

HEATED CONFRONTATION

Men, women and children living in the settlement gathered around the posse. Armed with hoes, rakes and clubs, they rallied behind Scipio Singleton, the acknowledged leader of the community. The residents resented the visit of law enforcement agents. Singleton inflamed the situation. He stated that no "white man" could arrest "one of their number" and threatened to shoot anyone who tried. Given the volatility of the situation, all members of the posse except Matthewes, Middleton and Van Ness fled. Holmes even left his cabin and pursued Smart Polite with a club, threatening to kill him. At that point, Matthewes intervened to rescue Polite and fired one barrel of his gun into the ground near Holmes's feet. While Holmes was unhurt, the bottoms of his pants were scorched. Holmes let Polite go and grabbed the gun from Matthewes's hands. Two of Holmes's compatriots then held Matthewes's arms. When finally released, Matthewes walked away from the men, raised his hand and cried, "Don't shoot me, you see I am unarmed." Despite the plea, Holmes deliberately shot Matthewes. The bullet entered the left side of the poor man's head above the ear. Matthewes collapsed dead on the ground. Middleton, a member of the posse, witnessed the shooting.

Van Ness had left the immediate area and so was not present for the fatal confrontation. Returning to the scene, he unknowingly stumbled over the body of Matthewes. Holmes waved his gun at Van Ness and shouted, "I killed him...and I'll kill you too." At that point, Van Ness pulled his gun and held Holmes at bay "until a cart could be brought from an adjoining plantation and the body taken home." After the incident, Scipio Singleton fled to Lady's Island and Holmes, asserting that he had fired in self-defense, surrendered to the authorities. The authorities held him and four others and only with difficulty protected them from workers on Matthewes's plantation, who wanted to take matters into their own hands. Local residents, incensed by the murder and the disorderly conduct of the DeSaussure residents,

Farmhouse, Port Royal, South Carolina, 1862. When possible, freedmen acquired land. *Courtesy of the Library of Congress, LC-B811-1177 [P&P] lot 4205.*

petitioned General Edward R.S. Canby, commander of the Second Military District (North and South Carolina), to have the settlers removed.

Harmon Van Ness, a native of New York, was the son-in-law of William Jenkins. A Civil War veteran, in 1870, Van Ness and his family lived with the Jenkins family. Van Ness worked in a phosphate plant. In 1880, Scipio Singleton was a laborer who lived in Lawton, Hampton County. John F. Porteous, a native of South Carolina and possibly the constable who deputized Matthewes, appears on the 1870 census of Charleston County as a government official. According to the 1870 census, Mick McGuire, Beaufort's Irish-born jailor, had Peter Holmes, the suspected thief, lodged in the Beaufort jail.

The Matthewes murder, of course, was not the only violence in the postwar years. For example, on November 24, 1876, the *New York Times* carried the account of another incident in Beaufort County. According to the paper, law officers had arrested eighteen African Americans who had attacked a constable and his posse at Stafford's Crossroads in Beaufort County.

CHAPTER 9
"Honor" among Thieves

The 1870s brought an end to Reconstruction in South Carolina. In 1876, white South Carolina Democrats reclaimed the statehouse and legislature. Former Confederate general Wade Hampton and his Red Shirts (armed rifle clubs that supported Wade Hampton and other Democratic candidates during the election of 1878), with ten thousand black votes, had restored white rule in the state. Hampton and his core supporters, the Bourbons, were Confederate veterans interested in turning back the clock to pre-secession days.

The 1870s, therefore, brought violence, intimidation and shame. With a black majority in the state and an active Republican Party, the only way to ensure a Hampton victory in 1876 was to "discourage" black voting. Despite federal oversight, voting fraud and intimidation were rife in many precincts. With close contests, for a time South Carolina had two governors and two Houses of Representatives. Eventually, a federal investigation recognized the Hampton election, and a new old era dawned in South Carolina and in Beaufort County. Yet with its black majority, African Americans continued to hold local political offices in Beaufort County into the twentieth century. Despite such vestiges of power, in parts of the county, life was fragile for black leaders. In November 1878, Benjamin Johnson, acting chair of a local Republican club, filed a deposition. By November, Johnson's home may have been in the newly formed Hampton County, which was cut out of old Beaufort District in February 1878. According to his story, Johnson was a victim of political persecution. In retaliation for his not joining the

Reflection of shrimp boats, dockside, St. Helena Island. Fish, shrimp and boats are integral parts of Beaufort life. *Ned Brown, photographer. Courtesy of the author.*

Democratic Party or supporting the Democratic ticket, on November 8, red-shirted mounted men burned his home, farm buildings and crops. As a result, he and his family fled to the town of Beaufort for safety.

A SPIN OF THE WHEEL

Racism, intimidation and voter fraud were not the only crimes in Beaufort during the 1870s. A murder in 1878 took Beaufort County sheriff William Wilson on a bizarre transcontinental chase. The case began simply. Two men, Peter Froman, a thirty-year-old native of the Netherlands, and F.W. Duncan jointly owned a flatboat at Beaufort. On this flatboat was a roulette wheel, and both men liked to gamble. During a "friendly" game on June 25, 1878, Froman lost heavily to Duncan and then obstinately refused to pay his gambling debt. An outraged Duncan went ashore and complained to the law. Obtaining a warrant for the arrest of Froman, Duncan and a constable returned to the boat and confronted an irate Froman. Froman adamantly refused to cooperate and shouted that he would kill anyone who approached him. When the constable attempted to perform his duty, Froman knocked the constable unconscious on the deck. Duncan then tried to disarm the angry Froman, at which point Froman threw Duncan overboard and allowed the hapless man to drown.

FLIGHT AND PURSUIT

At that point, Froman fled Beaufort before the crime was discovered. Arriving in the port of New Orleans, he signed on as a sailor on the *Crom Donkin*, which soon sailed for Liverpool. Given his preference for life at sea, it is probable that Peter Froman was by occupation and temperament a sailor. By the time Sheriff Wilson—a native of New York who had married a South Carolina woman and settled in Beaufort—arrived in New Orleans, Froman and the ship were at sea. Wilson then returned to South Carolina, secured the necessary paperwork and sailed for England, where he boarded Froman's ship off Gravesend. When Froman caught sight of the sheriff, he jumped overboard and tried to swim for shore. The crew of a small boat sent after him eventually, with great exertion, subdued the fugitive and returned him to the ship.

After the ship docked, Froman was taken to London and "arraigned in the Bow-Street Police Court." There, the court jailed Froman pending

Landing stage, Liverpool, England. In 1878, Beaufort fugitive Peter Froman joined the crew of a ship bound for Liverpool. *American Stereoscopic Company, c. 1900. Courtesy of the Library of Congress, LC-USZ62-118010.*

Steamship landing, Liverpool, England, circa 1901. In the fall of 1878, after an arduous trans-Atlantic chase, Beaufort Sheriff William Wilson and his prisoner, Peter Froman, sailed from England on the steamship *Nevada*. *Courtesy of the Library of Congress, LC-USZ62-68738.*

extradition. While incarcerated, Froman escaped from his cell and made his way to the roof of the jail. However, he was again recaptured with a violent struggle before he could rappel down to the street. Catching Froman was one challenge, but hanging onto him was another. He desperately wanted his freedom and seized every opportunity to escape.

WILSON GETS HIS MAN

Eventually, on October 26, 1878, Inspector Thornthwaite of Scotland Yard formally transferred custody of Peter Froman to Sheriff Wilson. Wilson and his captive boarded the steamship *Nevada* for the return trip. However, to prevent another escape attempt, Wilson placed Froman in irons. Arriving in New York, the ship entered quarantine. While in quarantine, Wilson telegraphed the New York police for assistance. Captain John Keely, a detective, answered the request. Keely, a native of Ireland, was thirty-five years of age in 1880. Wilson wanted officers sent to the Williams & Guion Steamship pier at King Street to assist in removing Froman. Two New York police officers boarded the *Nevada* and discovered Wilson and a "morose" chained Froman sharing a cabin.

Behind the Scenes

As bizarre as this story is, there is supporting documentation in the records of Governor Wade Hampton housed in the South Carolina Department of Archives and History. On August 22, 1878, acting United States secretary of state Frederick William Seward wrote Governor Hampton "reporting the arrest of Peter Froman." The letter stated that Froman had been a stowaway on the ship *Crom Donkin*, which sailed from Bull River to London. When apprehended, Froman had confessed to wounding a policeman and murdering "a white man" in Beaufort, South Carolina, prior to July 14, 1878. The acting secretary asked Hampton to verify the truthfulness of the confession and follow the detailed procedures to arrange for Froman's extradition. Earlier on

Tugboat, New York Harbor. In late 1878, Sheriff William Wilson and his reluctant captive safely arrived in New York Harbor. *H.C. White Co., c. 1905. Courtesy of the Library of Congress, LC-USZC2-6211.*

August 19, 1878, Minister Welsh of the United States Legation in London had brought the matter to the attention of Secretary of State William Maxell Evarts. Welsh had asked Evarts to telegraph immediately if extradition were desired and to "send officer, warrant and deposition."

William Maxwell Evarts (1818–1901) was United States secretary of state during the administration of President Rutherford B. Hayes. Evarts is perhaps better known for his defense of President Andrew Johnson during Johnson's impeachment. When Evarts died, numerous tributes appeared in *Public Opinion*. Many lauded his judicial judgment, his legal acumen and his wit. As one phrased it, Evarts was a "great lawyer, an able statesman, and a great character." Acting Secretary of State William Frederick Seward was the son of William Henry Seward, who had served as secretary of state under Presidents Abraham Lincoln and Andrew Johnson and survived an assassination attempt. In 1867, he purchased "Seward's Folly"—better known as Alaska—from Russia.

A MINOR MYSTERY

Sheriff Wilson was not the only Beaufort resident to visit New York City during the 1870s. Wilson's visit was possibly more successful than that of Martin M. Kingman. Kingman left Beaufort and arrived in New York City on November 18, 1879, carrying a large sum of cash in order to purchase jewelry for the "holiday trade." After his arrival, he lodged at the Astor Hotel. Planning to stay only two weeks, by December 7 Kingman had disappeared, and his worried family contacted authorities in New York. According to a published description, Kingman was five feet, four inches tall and when last seen was wearing an overcoat and carrying an umbrella. In 1870, Kingman, a native of Massachusetts, lived with his wife, Laura, in Beaufort. The 1870 census listed his occupation at that time as lumber merchant. This story, however, apparently had a happy ending. In 1880, Martin and his wife Laura were living on East Thirty-third Street in New York City. The lost was found and perhaps lived happily ever after.

CHAPTER 10
Conflict of Interest

Historically, the 1920s were known for Prohibition, speakeasies, bathtub gin, flappers and the Charleston. In Beaufort, the 1920s were known for scandal and murder. Within five years, at least three major controversies engulfed the city by the sea. The first controversy, in 1922, threatened public confidence in the sheriff of Beaufort County.

This controversy concerned the death of Thomas Leonard Perry Bettison, aka Betterson. Bettison died on August 9, 1922, from, according to his death certificate, "shock—caused by blow on head." The blow, possibly from the proverbial blunt instrument, fractured the skull of the sixty-eight-year-old man. By occupation, the widowed Bettison, a native of Barnwell County, was a painter and had lived in Beaufort for thirty-seven years. He was the son of T.L.P. and Ann Alexander Bettison. His brother A.P. Bettison of Allendale provided the information for Bettison's death certificate. In addition to A.P. Bettison, T.L.P. Bettison left two other brothers—Preston Bettison of Williston, South Carolina, and William Bettison of Mississippi.

The death of Bettison challenged the town of Beaufort, the impartiality of its law enforcement and the members of the Baptist Church of Beaufort. On August 10, 1922, *The State* newspaper carried an account of the incident. According to the newspaper, Bettison died during the afternoon of August 9 "while sitting in a chair in his living room." As testimony at the coroner's inquest was inconclusive, that assertion was later withdrawn. However, according to Dr. William B. Ryan of Coosawhatchie, who attended the wounded man, a blow to the head killed Bettison and Bettison did die in his own home.

Above: View of Beaufort from the bay, Beaufort Scenes 1925. The 1920s were challenging times for Beaufort residents. *The Christensen Family Paper, folder 46. Courtesy of the South Caroliniana Library, University of South Carolina, Columbia.*

Below: Bay Street, Beaufort, circa 1925. For much of Beaufort's history, Bay Street was the commercial center of town. An ill-fated confrontation on Bay Street in 1922 ended in a charge of murder. The defendant also operated a furniture store on Bay Street. *The Christensen Family Papers, folder 47. Courtesy of the South Caroliniana Library, University of South Carolina, Columbia.*

Convened that evening, a coroner's jury returned a verdict of death at the hands of Ralph E. Brown. According to testimony, Brown, his father B.S. Brown and Bettison had an acrimonious exchange the morning of August 9 that ended when Ralph Brown knocked down Bettison. The paper described Bettison as an older man with no family in Beaufort who had "lived for many years as an artisan." Brown, the accused perpetrator, was a "prominent young furniture dealer" whose family lived in Beaufort. Given the findings of the coroner's inquest, Sheriff J.H. Bailey took Brown into custody.

In 1920, the twenty-eight-year-old Brown and his wife, Olive, rented a house on Craven Street. The census listed his occupation as a "retail merchant" who sold furniture. Brown operated Brown Furniture Store on Bay Street in Beaufort. In 1920, according to the census, Sheriff James H. Bailey was a truck farmer who lived with his family in Bluffton.

PUBLIC OUTRAGE

Although Sheriff Bailey took Brown into custody, he did not incarcerate the accused murderer. Rather, contrary to the law, Bailey housed Brown overnight in the sheriff's home. Bailey's actions incensed Beaufort residents, who thought Bailey was giving Brown preferential treatment. When Bailey refused to jail Brown, concerned members of the public gathered at the Beaufort County Courthouse on August 11, the same day as Bettison's funeral. There, the assembled group appointed a three-man committee to "collect, prepare and present evidence against" the sheriff. During the proceedings, Brown's brother Wilbur Brown cast the only dissenting vote. Solicitor Randolph Murdaugh attended the meeting and shared information concerning Bailey's actions. Prior to the meeting, Bailey relented and jailed Brown but then refused to attend the public gathering or explain his actions. During the meeting, yet another potential conflict of interest emerged. A member of Brown's defense team was also the sheriff's legal advisor—C.M. Aman.

The citizens attending also criticized Beaufort city councilmen for their lenient treatment of Brown on earlier occasions and asked by a vote of eighty-nine to thirty-eight for three councilmen to resign. The Bettison-Brown-Bailey triangle caused widespread discontent about the citizenry. In addition to town leaders, many women also attended the public meeting and voted. Senator Niels Christensen chaired the meeting and Alan Paul served as secretary. J.H. Bellamy and William Altman moved that the group

Former Beaufort County Courthouse. Originally built in 1884, the county completely remodeled the courthouse in 1936. Several of the cases from the 1920s had their day in court here. Also, in 1922, irate citizens held a mass meeting here to protest Sheriff James H. Bailey's handling of the Bettison-Brown case. *Courtesy of Jacob Helsley.*

appoint a committee to meet with the sheriff. The motion carried, and the attendees elected the following to serve: L.H. Hall, jeweler, Alan Paul and Gus Sanders. At the time, Sanders served as treasurer of Beaufort County.

On August 22, Senator Christensen of the citizens' committee announced the members of a three-man committee appointed as a result of a resolution approved during the mass meeting to "prefer charges" against the sheriff. Members of that committee were Benjamin Bostick, Pat Wall and Dr. E.C.B. Mole. Bostick of Beaufort was a veteran of World War I and employed as a truck farmer. Wall, a resident of Port Royal, managed a truck farm at Sheldon. Dr. Mole was a physician from Hardeeville. In describing the committee and their mission, Christensen stated, "They have accepted appointment from a citizens' meeting that was representative in numbers and character of Beaufort and its surrounding county."

BAILEY'S DEFENSE

Sheriff Bailey, although not up for reelection for two years, alleged in a statement published in the *Beaufort Gazette* on August 25, 1922, that his opponents who masterminded the mass meeting were political opportunists and the Bettison murder "case simply furnished an opportunity to get certain men in the limelight." Defending his actions, Bailey cited the "hysterical" state of Brown's wife as a factor in his decision to keep the accused under "his personal guard" in his home. Bailey continued his defense by attacking the importance of the deceased and the motivation of the protestors. As he wrote, "Nobody here cared anything about Bettison. He was an old man that meant little to the business world and absolutely nothing in the world to the men who are and were behind the movement." Concerning a possible conflict of interest with his legal advisor Aman representing Brown, the sheriff tersely noted, "Aman can take care of himself." Bailey did acknowledge that he regretted the "incident."

Brown, claiming self-defense, did secure bond and was released after he posted $3,000. As a result of the mass meeting, the citizens' committee asked all members of the Beaufort City Council, including Mayor Albert J. Kinghorn to resign. In addition, the committee made the same request of the city police force, including Chief Lee B. Simpson (a native of Georgia). According to an article published August 22 in *The State*, only one councilman, David Mittle, owner of and salesman for the bottling works, had resigned.

Brown's Trial

Brown's trial opened on December 8, 1922—the same day that the grand jury indicted J.H. Bailey for "misconduct in office." Solicitor Randolph Murdaugh prosecuted the Brown case. George Warren, Mendel L. Smith (who was also involved in the defense of Walter E. Richardson in Chapter 7) and C.M. Aman represented Brown. Assisting with Brown's defense were attorneys William Levin, George W. Beckett and Heyward Jenkins.

The court spent two hours selecting a jury. The jury included the following men: J.C. O'Quinn, A.B. Lubkin, J.B. Bailey, C.R. Richardson, M.C. Smith, M.S. Lipsitz, M. Levin, John Brabham, E.L. Allen, W.L. Beach, E. White and J.D. Beverly. Murdaugh called as his first witness Dr. M.G. Elliott, who had performed the autopsy on Bettison. Frederick Christensen testified concerning the incident on Bay Street involving the two men that occurred the morning of Bettison's death. Mrs. J.B. Evans testified that she had observed Brown twice heading in the direction of Bettison's house. Bettison's neighbor, Eliza Washington, who lived across the street from the deceased, also testified that Brown had visited Bettison twice on the day Bettison died. In addition, R.V. Bray stated that Brown had called him saying that Bettison was unconscious. Later recalled to the stand, Bray identified a hoe that had been found in Bettison's room.

The defense argued self-defense and produced several witnesses such as W.A. McDaniel and Wilbur Brown who testified that neither Bettison nor Brown was drinking at the time of Bettison's death. Dr. W.B. Ryan testified that Brown had summoned him to attend the wounded Bettison. According to Ryan, he found Bettison sitting in a chair and bandaged his head wound. While the doctor was seeking help to move Bettison to his bed, the injured man died. Ryan stated that Brown had paid for Bettison's care.

B.S. Brown, father of the defendant, presented his version of the earlier altercation on Bay Street. According to B.S. Brown, he called Bettison "a very vile name," and Bettison struck him. At that point, the younger Brown pushed Bettison into the street. B.S. Brown also acknowledged that he had sent his son to "clear up" the matter with Bettison. Ralph E. Brown also took the stand and testified that while he had "struck the fatal blow," he had acted in self-defense. In his summation, Solicitor Murdaugh ridiculed the idea of self-defense.

Nevertheless, at the conclusion of testimony on Friday, December 9, the jury, after a short deliberation, acquitted Brown of the more serious crime of murder. However, the jury did convict Brown of carrying a "concealed weapon" and sentenced him to thirty days in jail suspended for "good behavior." With his name legally cleared, Brown attempted unsuccessfully to resume his retail business in Beaufort.

AFTERWARD

According to *A Lamp Unto the Lowcountry*, members of the Baptist Church of Beaufort buried the indigent Bettison, who like Richard V. Bray was a member of the Baraca Sunday school class, in the church graveyard and published a resolution on his death in the *Beaufort Gazette*. The congregation, however, had difficulty with Brown's role in the incident and in January 1923 "withdrew fellowship" from Ralph E. Brown.

In turn, Ralph E. Brown left Beaufort and moved to Florida. Until his death in 1938, Brown worked for the Seminole Furniture Company in Tampa, Florida. Only forty-six years of age when he died, Brown left a

The Baptist Church of Beaufort, circa 1940. Both the victim and the accused in the Bettison-Brown affair were members of the Baptist Church of Beaufort. T.L.P. Bettison, the victim, was buried in the church cemetery. *Courtesy of the South Caroliniana Library, University of South Carolina, Columbia, WPA-PL-BFT-B-6-1.*

widow, Edith Brown. The Reverend Wallace Cliff conducted his funeral at Tampa Heights Presbyterian Church.

Sheriff James Henry Bailey survived the incident and lived as a contractor and farmer in the Gray's Hill area of Beaufort County. A native of Bluffton, Bailey served only one term as sheriff of Beaufort County (1920–24). After a long and successful life, he died in 1960, leaving a large family.

CHAPTER 11

Chivalry—Beaufort Style

The 1920s in Beaufort were filled with headlines and stories. In 1923, one of those stories stirred the hearts of all defenders of southern womanhood. It brought a leading layman in the Baptist Church of Beaufort to the federal prison in Atlanta and aroused the citizenry of Beaufort to elect the accused mayor.

THE CONFLICT

In 1920, according to the census, Richard Van Bray was a thirty-six-year-old truck farmer. He and his wife, Jane, and their two children rented a house on New Street. By 1930, the Bray family lived on East Street in Beaufort. Bray and his family were active members of the Baptist Church of Beaufort.

The story began, according to the records of the Circuit Court of Appeals, Fourth Circuit, *Bray v. United States* 289 F. 329 (1923), when a federal agent of the Internal Revenue Service came to Beaufort. Agent George W. Smith was investigating the estate of George Waterhouse, the father of Jane Bray. At the invitation of Walter E. Richardson (who will figure prominently in Chapter 11), Smith visited Richardson in his office at the Beaufort Bank. At that time, Richardson was president of the Beaufort Bank. During the course of their conversation, Bray also called on Richardson. Although Smith offered to excuse himself, Richardson asked him to stay. Richardson

Originally built to house the United States Post Office, in 1934 this building became Columbia City Hall. Prior to that time, the Internal Revenue Service had offices on the second floor of this building. Art Work of Columbia, *part 2. Courtesy of the South Caroliniana Library, University of South Carolina, Columbia.*

then introduced Bray as a relative of the deceased by marriage and, as such, an interested party in Smith's inquiry. Following the introductions, the three men sat around a table discussing the estate in question.

During that conversation, Smith pointedly asked about the rent produced by a piece of real estate in which Waterhouse had a half interest. Richardson deferred to Bray for an answer. However, both Richardson and Bray found Smith's questions probing and unsettling. At that point, both refused to provide specific answers as to the nature of the rent collected on the property. Bray's response to the agent included the words, "You don't seem to believe what I tell you." Irritated with Bray and Richardson's lack of cooperation, Smith then reminded them of his legal authority to compel their cooperation. At that point, as Smith shifted in his seat, Bray hit him. Smith fell, and the two men struggled on the floor. Bray, the larger man, held Smith down even though Smith begged him to quit. At one point, Bray picked up an armchair to throw at Smith, but Richardson intervened. Eventually, Smith escaped from Bray and, with difficulty, ran from the bank.

Bray's version of the dispute differed from the synopsis found in the case held in the Fourth Circuit of Appeals. According to the *Beaufort Gazette* of November 23, 1923, Bray contended that the dispute was a result of his "chivalrous action in defending a Beaufort lady when a disparaging remark was made to her by an income tax expert."

Regardless, Bray was charged with "assaulting a revenue officer" in violation of the United States code. During the trial, Bray testified on his own behalf and admitted his actions. However, in the course of Bray's defense, comments were made that painted the IRS agent as a "coward" and a Yankee (as he was from Boston), while Bray was a "red-blooded man" and a southern gentleman "resenting an insult." From other sources, it appears that Bray considered Smith's remarks insulting to his mother-in-law, the widow of George Waterhouse.

In his charge to the jury, the presiding judge, Henry A. Middleton Smith, acknowledged the rhetorical similarities presented by the defense with the *code duello*. However, he noted that in the case of a duel, one man notified the other before the conflict, while in this instance Bray had attacked a federal official performing his job. According to the appeal, the judge spoke thusly to the jury: "This fellow Smith may be a coward; but a coward has a right to live and perform his duties. And he is not to be beaten up by a bully or a swashbuckler, because he is a coward." The judge subsequently clarified his meaning: "I said that the argument that a man is justified in beating another man under the circumstances of this case and insulting him would be to style such a one a bully and a swashbuckler."

THE COURT DECISION

The jury found R.V. Bray Jr. guilty under section 65 of the Criminal Code (Comp. St. Sec. 10233), assaulting "an officer of the internal revenue in the execution of his duty," but recommended mercy. The judge sentenced him to serve one year in the federal penitentiary in Atlanta and to pay a fine of $1,000 plus court costs. Bray's attorney, J. Waties Waring, appealed the decision. Assistant United States attorney Louis M. Shimel represented the United States. On May 1, 1923, the Circuit Court of Appeals, Fourth Circuit (289 F. 329), with one dissenting justice, upheld the original verdict. The court found that "no legally material fact is in dispute," as Bray's testimony agreed with that of the government witnesses. The appeal addressed several issues, including the trial judge's charge to the jury and the fact that trying the case in federal court precluded a conviction for simple assault, a lesser crime with a possible fine of $100 or less. The majority of the judges on appeal upheld the lower court's ruling and sentence. Judge Waddill in his dissent stated that the lower court erred "in taking from the jury the determination of the character of the assault committed." Waddill also wrote, "I cannot give my assent to the affirmance of a judgment that would impose upon a peaceable and orderly citizen and business man of good standing in the community in which he lived the serious consequences that would follow therefrom, for an affair of such trivial character as shown by the testimony even when taken most unfavorably against the accused."

Of historical note, J. Waties Waring later served as a federal judge. In 1941, President Franklin D. Roosevelt nominated Waring to the federal judiciary. As a judge in the United States District Court for the Eastern District of South Carolina, Waring heard *Briggs v. Elliott*, one of the school desegregation cases later heard by the United States Supreme Court as *Brown v. Board of Education of Topeka, Kansas*. In his dissent for the Briggs case, Waring used the phrase "separate educational facilities are inherently unequal." When the United States Supreme Court later issued its landmark ruling in the Brown case, the decision included that now famous phrase.

The Mayoral Election

Following his conviction but while the case was on appeal, the voters of Beaufort elected Bray mayor by a vote of 247 to 94. Notwithstanding the margin of victory, Bray faced serious consequences. With his appeals denied in May 1923, Bray's supporters traveled to Washington, D.C., seeking presidential clemency for Bray. Members of the delegation to Washington were W.J. Thomas, Walter E. Richardson, Mary Waterhouse, Mrs. George Waterhouse, the Reverend Mr. F. Clyde Helms (pastor of the Baptist Church of Beaufort), Senator Niels Christensen and J. Fraser Lyon. President Warren G. Harding refused the petition.

Consequently, in June 1923, Bray turned himself in to the United States marshal's office in Charleston. Bray surrendered to United States marshal Leaphart. Shortly thereafter, Bray, with Deputy Marshal J.O. Lea, left Charleston at 5:15 p.m. for Atlanta. Accompanying Bray to Charleston was a group of prominent citizens representing the city of Beaufort, the county of Beaufort and Beaufort's commercial interests, as well as personal friends. The group included T. Craven, chair of the Beaufort County Democratic Executive Committee; F.B. Wells, Young Men's Board of Trade; J.F. Morrall, Beaufort Chamber of Commerce; J.C. Spark, Beaufort town council; and Senator Niels Christensen, representing Beaufort County. In addition, Bray's friends J. Heyward Jenkins, J.B. Keyserling, Walter Barwick, J.B. Wall and Homer Young joined the group demonstrating their support for Mayor Bray.

While in prison, Bray continued to perform his duties as mayor. The *Beaufort Gazette* of August 24, 1923, carried a letter from Mayor Bray to the people of Beaufort. In his letter, Bray commented that it was "more or less an awful hardship to be away from my family and friends in old Beaufort." Nevertheless, he hastened to reassure his family and friends, "I am not a criminal and never was one, and serving a year in this prison will never make me one." Bray also commented on his new sewing skills (he was learning to sew on buttons) and his prison responsibilities. Bray drove the mail truck and, as such, while pursuing his responsibilities, was trusted to leave the prison and drive around Atlanta. He closed his letter by commending the work of the new city manager and encouraging Beaufort residents to work together. Bray wanted a "clean and impartial government" for Beaufort.

HOME AGAIN

After Harding's death on August 2, 1923, Calvin Coolidge became president. On November 23, 1923, the new president pardoned Bray. South Carolina congressman James F. Byrnes and United States senator Nathaniel Barksdale Dial worked actively to secure Bray's release.

As the pardon was immediately effective, Bray, having served about half of his sentence, left Atlanta on Wednesday and arrived in Beaufort on Thursday. The city's mayor was once again home in Beaufort. As Judge James Thomas later remembered, a band greeted Bray upon his return from prison, but that story is unverified. News coverage suggests a less dramatic return. Bray had no comment about his ordeal but did walk around Beaufort with "a happy smile." Nonetheless, Bray's early release ensured that he would be on hand for Beaufort's greatest challenge of the 1920s, the failure of the Beaufort Bank.

After his terms as mayor, Bray served six years as supervisor of Beaufort County. A mason, Bray was active in civic life and also served as a member

Built in 1844, the Baptist Church of Beaufort is one of Beaufort's historic churches. Mayor Richard Van Bray and his wife were active members of the church and are buried in the churchyard. *Ned Brown, photographer, c. 1960. Courtesy of Dr. George A. Jones.*

of the Public Service Commission. He and his wife, Jane Waterhouse Bray, were active members of the Baptist Church of Beaufort and are buried in the church's graveyard. In 1939, when Bray died in Savannah, Dr. Warren M. Seay, pastor of the Baptist Church, conducted his funeral.

Born in Richland County, South Carolina, Bray left one son, Richard V. Bray, when he died. His obituary praised Bray as a "friend to everybody," a man whose "word was his bond" and a "valuable citizen."Among the honorary pallbearers were such Beaufort notables as Calhoun Thomas, W.J. Thomas Sr., W.B. Harvey, Sheriff J.E. McTeer, David R. Schein, F.H. Christensen and Howard E. Danner. With such a send-off, it appears that Bray's quixotic engagement with the revenue agent had little impact on his subsequent life and career in Beaufort.

CHAPTER 12

House of Cards

The third and perhaps greatest calamity of 1920s Beaufort was the devastating banking scandal of 1926–27. The alleged perpetrator of an elaborate scheme of false representation and fraud was Walter E. Richardson, who was also present for Bray's attack on the revenue agent and who lobbied in Washington for Bray's release. These stories from the 1920s demonstrate clearly the interconnectedness of Beaufort's leadership. Beaufort was a small town, and its elite pursued similar aims, met frequently and interacted in a restricted arena. Family ties were widespread and important.

The bank story begins innocently enough on Thursday, Christmas Eve 1908. A front-page story in the *Beaufort Gazette* trumpeted the organization of the Beaufort Bank. Those attending the organizational meeting subscribed $33,500 in stock and chose the following to serve as directors of the bank: J.M. Lengnick, John N. Wallace, Charles E. Danner, Charles G. Luther, William J. Thomas, George Waterhouse, Randolph R. Legare, M.S. Epstein, Walter E. Richardson, C.O. Townsend and P.H. Christensen. After the organizational meeting was adjourned, the newly elected directors selected the following officers: William J. Thomas, president; George Waterhouse, vice-president; and Walter E. Richardson, cashier.

The board of directors was a veritable who's who of prominent Beaufort citizens. For example, William J. Thomas, born in Tennessee, was a forty-seven-year-old lawyer; Charles G. Luther, a native of New York, operated a retail mercantile and drugstore (Luther's Pharmacy); Charles E. Danner

Beaufort Bank building, Bay Street, Beaufort, South Carolina. Incorporated April 1, 1909, the Beaufort Bank abruptly closed on Saturday, July 10, 1926, triggering court cases, financial losses and recriminations. In 1912, W.J. Thomas was president of the bank and W.E. Richardson was cashier. *Courtesy of Jacob Helsley.*

was the proprietor of Charles E. Danner & Company on Bay Street; John N. Wallace was a dry goods merchant; and Randolph R. Legare was a retail merchant who sold plantation supplies.

Walter E. Richardson, the new cashier, also had local connections. He had lived many years in Beaufort with his father, Dr. C.G. Richardson. He was also a successful banker. In 1908, Richardson was cashier of the Bank of Hampton, president of the Planters & Merchants Bank of Varnville and one of the organizers of the Bank of Estill. The press notice concluded with these prophetic words: "Those who know of his [Richardson's] record have great confidence in his ability and integrity."

In 1910, Walter E. Richardson was twenty years old and lived with his wife, Lucy C., in Ward 4 of the city of Beaufort. The Richardsons were relative newlyweds, as they had only been married eleven months when enumerated on April 20 for the 1910 census. By 1920, Walter and Lucy Richardson had two children.

In 1914, Richardson survived an effort to replace him as a receiver for the Bank of Brunson (Supreme Court of South Carolina *Ex Parte Faust et al. Rhame v. Bank of Brunson*, 96 S.C. 411, 81 S.E. 7, 1914). B.J. Rhame, the state bank examiner, and I.P. Faust with others, executors of H. Ginn, petitioned to remove Richardson from the receivership of the insolvent Bank of Brunson because Richardson worked in Beaufort, fifty miles from Brunson, and was an official with the Beaufort Bank and other banks. In addition, Richardson was a receiver for the Carolina Telephone Company. The Bank of Brunson held a contested mortgage executed by the Carolina Telephone Company. These relationships, according to the plaintiffs, constituted a conflict of interest. The lower court judge ruled that Richardson could perform his responsibilities. On appeal, the Supreme Court upheld the decision.

The vision of a man of integrity clashed with reality on Saturday, July 10, 1926, when the Beaufort Bank failed. This catastrophe destroyed public confidence, eradicated savings and left many disturbed depositors and perplexed onlookers. Efforts to unravel the situation and identify causes and responsible agents occupied many months.

Initially, the closing of the Beaufort Bank had a domino effect, as the Bank of Yemassee closed as well. Fortunately, the Bank of Yemassee was able to reopen. Before the banking catastrophe, Beaufort County had three banks: the Beaufort Bank, the Bank of Yemassee and the Peoples Bank.

Bay Street with the Peoples Bank, Beaufort South Carolina. Although the Peoples Bank building burned in the great fire of 1907, the Peoples Bank as a banking entity was one of two Beaufort County state banks that survived the banking scandal of 1926–27. Incorporated in 1902, F.W. Scheper was president of the bank in 1912 and W.F. Marscher was cashier. *Courtesy of the Beaufort County Library.*

After July 1926, only two of those banks survived. Given the economic clout of banks, losing even one had a deleterious impact on the financial climate of Beaufort County.

In July 1926, the directors of the Beaufort Bank, according to *Gray v. Thomas et al.* 163 S.C. 421, 161 S.E. 743 (1931), realizing its precarious condition, petitioned the state bank examiner to take over the bank for thirty days. Accordingly, on Monday, July 12, 1926, the state bank examiner assumed control of the bank "pursuant to the provisions of section 3981, volume 3, Code 1922." On August 10, the state examiner appointed well-known Beaufort attorney W.J. Thomas as receiver of the Beaufort Bank. Thomas proceeded to liquidate the bank's assets.

According to South Carolina Supreme Court case *Gray v. Thomas*, during the time that the state bank examiner controlled the bank and before the appointment of Thomas as receiver, bank officials, stockholders and community supporters met to plan how to raise funds in order to reopen the bank. While several meetings occurred, according to later court testimony, no minutes of any of these meetings are available. Subsequent oral recollections document different opinions and proposals. Regardless, those at the meetings did appoint committees to "solicit and collect funds and securities to finance the reopening of the bank." Richard V. Bray and J.R. Bellamy were named "trustees to receive and hold" any monies or securities collected. According to the *Beaufort Gazette* of August 5, the stockholders also issued a public statement that the bank would reopen when it had $200,000 in deposits and agreement from the present depositors to leave their money in the bank for five years if needed. This notice claimed that the bank had the $200,000 pledged but needed the support of its depositors. The notice appears to vary somewhat with the court records.

In support of the effort, J.W. Gray pledged $10,000 underwritten by a mortgage on real estate he owned. In return for his subscription, when the bank reopened, bank representatives promised Gray and the other subscribers certificates of deposit in the amount of their subscription. That meant that Gray's note and mortgage would be exchanged for a certificate of deposit when the bank reopened. So on August 5, Gray executed the note and mortgage in question and left the documents with his attorney, W.J. Thomas, who was also a bank stockholder and officer. The following day, or shortly thereafter, J.R. Bellamy and N.P. Bryan gave R.C. Horne Jr. $104,000 in securities, including Gray's note and mortgage. The identity of the person who authorized the transfer is not known.

The Beaufort Bank owed the Hanover National Bank of New York in the neighborhood of $75,000. To secure its loan, the Hanover Bank held a note and collaterals valued at $200,000 from the Beaufort Bank. According to Horne's testimony, he was delegated to use the subscriptions to pay the Hanover Bank so that bank would release the collaterals that belonged to the Beaufort Bank. The Hanover Bank planned to sell the collaterals on August 12.

As part of the plan, Horne went to Detroit in an attempt to gain Edwin Denby's assistance with this project. Denby was a respected Michigan attorney, former United States congressman and former secretary of the navy under President Warren G. Harding. From 1919 to 1928, he also owned the Robert Means house on Bay Street in Beaufort. Before embarking on his mission, Horne obtained from W.W. Bradley of the State Bank Examiner's office a statement that the Beaufort Bank did not own any of the recently pledged securities but that their owners had agreed to their use to rescue the bank. Horne's initial negotiations with Denby were not successful. However, Denby's law partner, J.J. Kennedy, suggested that Horne try for $25,000 rather than the desired $75,000. In the end, Horne allegedly paid the New York bank $25,000 but did not secure the release of the needed collaterals. To secure the $25,000 loan, Denby ended up with $30,000 in securities signed by Richardson as president of the Beaufort Bank. Included in that assignment were Gray's note and mortgage. Despite these efforts, the Beaufort Bank never reopened.

Gray, surprised by this turn of events, moved to have his mortgage canceled and the note declared null and void. Gray sued Thomas and Denby. A special referee upheld Denby's right to the securities. Yet Judge M.L. Bonham, Court of Common Pleas, Beaufort Circuit, reviewed the findings of H. Klugh Purdy, the special referee, and found "numerous exceptions." For example, Bonham found that Richardson had no authority to assign securities that did not belong to the bank. Under the fundraising agreement, the subscriptions were only due when the bank reopened and issued certificates of deposit for the monies pledged. As that never happened, the bank did not acquire title to Gray's note and mortgage, so Gray's mortgage and note were invalid. In addition, Bonham noted that "it would be an insult to his [Denby's] reputation and attainments to suggest that he did not know the laws of South Carolina as they pertain to insolvent banks in the hands of the state bank examiner." Therefore, Denby knew that Richardson could "not legally execute the note" that he accepted from Horne.

In concluding his opinion, Bonham commented, "It seems hard that Mr. Denby should suffer because of his kindly feeling for Beaufort, but it would be harder to make Mr. Gray suffer." Consequently, Bonham sustained the exceptions to the special referee's report and ordered Denby to deliver Gray's note to the Beaufort County clerk of court, "who shall mark the mortgage satisfied…and shall deliver the mortgage, with the note, to the plaintiff J.W. Gray, or his attorney."

The defendants in the action appealed Bonham's decision. However, on December 10, 1931, the South Carolina Supreme Court upheld Bonham's ruling. Unfortunately, Denby, who died in 1929, did not live to see the final resolution of the case.

On October 3, 1927, William J. Thomas, attorney and receiver of the Beaufort Bank, sold bank property at public auction. The role of a receiver is to protect and administer assets. Thomas sold four pieces of property of the defunct bank: the Beaufort Bank building, which was purchased by Peoples Securities Company of Charleston; a lot on the bluff, which was knocked down to C.L. Baxter; the Palace Market building, which was sold to Calhoun Thomas, a Beaufort attorney; and property on Depot Road, which was bought by Christensen Realty Company.

The failure of the Beaufort Bank affected depositors and creditors. The case of R.T.W. Richards illustrated the complexity of the situation. Richards had borrowed money from the Beaufort Bank and paid off his note by check on the due date. Unfortunately for Richards, according to his account, he paid off the note in June and the bank closed in July. Consequently, he never received a receipt for his payment or his cancelled note, and the only witnesses to the transaction were Richards and W.P. Jay, former cashier of the Beaufort Bank. Instead of receiving acknowledgement that his debt had been paid, the Bank of Columbia, to whom the note had been pledged as collateral for a debt, sued Richards. In December 1926, Judge T.J. Mauldin ruled in favor of the Intermediate Credit Bank, and Richards was ordered to pay off the note again.

The *Beaufort Gazette* of February 11, 1927, reported that the Hampton County Grand Jury had indicted Walter E. Richardson, president of the defunct Bank of Hampton, with violating section 258 of the South Carolina Code. The grand jury, however, did not indict John S. Williams, vice-president of the bank. Similarly, they did not indict S.E. Ulmer, cashier, and H.M. Preacher, director, Merchants & Planters Bank of Brunson; W.V. Bowers cashier, Planters & Merchants Bank of Varnville; or R.A. Anderson, cashier, Bank of Hampton. Specifically, the grand jury charged Richardson with borrowing "in excess of one-tenth of the capital stock of the bank of which he is an officer or director."

On February 18, 1927, Beaufort mayor Richard V. Bray Jr. wrote an open letter to the editor of the *Beaufort Gazette*. In this letter, Bray complained of the lack of action following the closing of the Beaufort Bank "more than seven months" ago. Bray also intimated that the newspaper editor feared to print the truth. The editor defended his position, contending that he had been unable to learn any additional information. For example, he had not received the expected auditors' report that had been promised in January. The editor also suggested that it was time for Beaufort to move forward and "start over again."

INDICTMENTS

On October 13, 1927, the *Beaufort Gazette* reported eleven indictments in the United States District Court in Charleston. Those indicted for "Conspiracy to violate provisions of the Federal Loan Act," including making false representations to the Federal Intermediate Credit Bank concerning loan securities, were Walter E. Richardson, Richard C. Horne Jr., Beulah Harvey, H.B. Macklin, E.B. Mitchell, Harry Bowers, Patrick Wall, J.L. Butler, W.R. Eve Jr., J. Sims and N.P. Bryan.

The court set the highest bond for Richardson and Horne. The total amount of money involved in the alleged fraudulent transactions was between $800,000 and $1 million. The indictments were the culmination of a yearlong investigation by Clifford Cagle and T.A. Donaldson of the Federal Bureau of Investigation into the affairs of the Beaufort Bank and the South Carolina Agricultural Credit Association. Both institutions closed on July 10, 1926. Judge Ernest F. Cochran set bond for Richardson and Horne at $24,000 each and Beulah Harvey $18,000. Bond for the others indicted ranged from $4,000 to $12,000.

As the city of Beaufort grappled with this catastrophe, a newspaper editor wrote on December 29, 1927, concerning the "great calamity" that had befallen Beaufort with the "failure of the Beaufort Bank" in 1926. In detailing the impact of the calamity, the editor asserted that before the bank's failure, Beaufort had been the "best, most well-to-do section of South Carolina." However, since the closing, many had "felt the touch of poverty," and others had left the city in desperation. According to the editorial, a Beaufort grand jury in the spring of 1927 had returned indictments against bank officials and others with business connections with the bank. Yet in the ensuing months there had been no trial and no resolution of the case. Instead, the defendants had requested and been granted a new venue in a neighboring city. Consequently, the editor lamented, nothing had been done to remove "the blight cast over the community" by the bank's failure.

As defendants and prosecutors scrambled for evidence, the scene at the bank building resembled moving day. The federal court referee W.D. Connor; F.S. Hughes, receiver of W.E. Richardson, former president of the bank; and S.T. Everett, receiver of the South Carolina Agricultural Credit Association, had subpoenaed all records of the Beaufort Bank and the Truckers Supply Company. W.J. Thomas, receiver of the Beaufort Bank and trustee of Truckers Supply Company, worked with bookkeeper Edward Nelson to box the records for transfer to United States District Court in Columbia. In all, six carloads of records traveled from Beaufort to Columbia for the trial.

BEFORE THE BAR

The trial commenced on Monday, January 9, 1928, with empanelling of a jury. Judge Ernest F. Cochran presided. The defendants in the case were W.E. Richardson, director of the South Carolina Agricultural Credit Association; Richard C. Horne Jr., president of the association; Beulah Harvey, secretary/treasurer of the association; N.P. Bryan, vice-president of the Truckers Supply Company; H.B. Macklin, director of the Truckers Supply Company and a New York commission agent; W.R. Eve Jr., general manager and treasurer of the Seaboard Farms of Ambrose, Georgia; and Harry Bowers, who had financial connections with Richardson, Horne and Harvey. Most of the defendants were Beaufort residents. In addition to Richardson, in 1920, for example, according to the census, Richard C. Horne Jr., a native of Missouri, was president of the America Ship Building Company; Beulah Harvey was a bank stenographer; and W.R. Eve Jr. was a truck farmer. Ed B. Mitchell was a farmer from Sheldon.

Members of the jury were E.F. Blewer, R.E. Howle, Gadsden Smith, H.W. McCollum, H.G. Fishburne, J.M. Hook Jr., J. Ben Smith, J.Q. Eargle, Roland Lide and H.W. Fuseler, foreman. During the trial, members of the jury were sequestered in the Jefferson Hotel in Columbia. Attorneys for the defendants were Edgar A. Brown, Alfred Huger, Robert L. Travis, R.A. Moore and Mendel L. Smith.

Lobby of the Jefferson Hotel, Columbia, South Carolina, circa 1915. Scene of a scuffle between Walter E. Richardson, president of the defunct Beaufort Bank, and one of the prosecution witnesses during the trial of Richardson and others for bank fraud. *Acmegraph Co., Chicago. Courtesy of William E. Benton.*

H.C. Arnold, president of the Federal Intermediate Credit Bank of Columbia, was the first witness. Arnold testified to transactions between the Credit Bank and Walter E. Richardson. The *Beaufort Gazette* quoted Arnold as stating during his two days of testimony that after the failure of the Beaufort Bank, Arnold had asked Richardson about the money that had been "deposited for the farmers of Beaufort district." Richardson's reply was, "It went to save the bank." Arnold then asked, "Then why wasn't the bank saved?" To the latter question, Richardson had no response. Many Beaufort depositors and investors also wondered why the bank had failed.

On January 19, 1928, the *Beaufort Gazette* carried a sensational revelation. F.H. Daniel, manager of the Federal Farm Loan and Intermediate Credit Bank of Columbia testified that Walter E. Richardson had told him that "he was assured by his maker that any wrong he [Richardson] should do would be offset by the good it would do for his community." According to Daniel, low prices and poor crops had created a crisis for the Beaufort Bank. Richardson prayed for divine guidance to rescue the bank and the South Carolina Agricultural Credit Association. The answer, according to conversation between Daniel and Richardson, was the Federal Intermediate Bank in Columbia. Despite efforts by the defense, Daniel stood fast in his statements. The defense counsel also sought, without success, to prove collusion between Arnold, who had testified earlier, and Richardson. Daniel's testimony also highlighted a number of irregularities with the accounts of the Beaufort Bank. Arnold and Daniel were only two of the one hundred listed government witnesses.

Melodrama interrupted the federal court proceedings as the January 26 *Beaufort Gazette* reported that a government witness had allegedly attacked Richard C. Horne Jr., one of the defendants, in the lobby of the Jefferson Hotel in Columbia. Travis, attorney for the defense, also reported that W.J. Thomas, a leading Beaufort attorney, had been knocked to the floor as he tried to separate the two men.

A key material witness for the prosecution was Edward Nelson. During his eight years as an employee of the Beaufort Bank, Nelson had risen from janitor to assistant bookkeeper and teller. Nelson's testimony documented altered balance sheets, such as an overdraft of $128,088.14 appearing in Harvey's records as a $6,131.21 balance. In addition, attorney W.J. Thomas, receiver of the Beaufort Bank and former president of the bank, testified that until a few hours before the bank closed, he was not aware of the bank's difficulties. Thomas and family connections lost more than $10,000 when the bank closed. Prior to the bank closing, Thomas and Richardson, bank cashier, had disagreed about bank policies, and Thomas had resigned.

RICHARDSON FOR THE DEFENSE

In his defense, Richardson testified that H.C. Arnold, president of the Federal Intermediate Credit Bank, was aware of and supported his business practices. He also alleged that as the South Carolina Agricultural Credit Association was a pioneer in offering such services, he did not have proper forms and, as he was not familiar with the federal farm loan legislation, had to rely upon the advice of Arnold and others. He defended Harvey's actions, as she was only the Credit Association's secretary and was not trained as a bookkeeper. On the stand, Richardson stressed his banking credentials as president of the Bank of Yemassee, the Farmers and Merchants Bank of Barnwell, the Bank of Hampton and the Merchants & Planters Bank of Brunson.

According to Richardson, the Credit Association made loans not only in South Carolina but also in North Carolina, Georgia, Texas and Virginia. However, by the end of 1925, the company had thousands of dollars in notes that were uncollectable. At that point, although the Beaufort Bank had advanced between $150,000 and $200,000 in the past to enable the association to satisfy notes due to the Federal Intermediate Credit Bank, in 1926 the Beaufort Bank was no longer in a position to do so. Consequently, the South Carolina Agricultural Credit Association could not pay the roughly $400,000 or $500,000 that was due the Columbia institution.

JUDGMENT AND SENTENCE

After a trial that lasted thirty-two days, the government rested its case, and on February 16, 1928, the defendants were found guilty. Judge Ernest F. Cochran of the United States District Court sentenced Walter E. Richardson, president of the Beaufort Bank and director of the South Carolina Agricultural Credit Company, and Richard C. Horne Jr., president of the South Carolina Agricultural Credit Company, to serve two years in the federal penitentiary in Atlanta. The court also sentenced Beulah B. Harvey, secretary of the South Carolina Agricultural Credit Association, to serve six months in the Aiken County jail.

Stating that he found fines in such instances "entirely inadequate as punishments," Judge Cochran also averred that only the "magnitude of the transactions" compelled him to impose the maximum possible sentence. Cochran, however, reserved the right to suspend Harvey's sentence at a later time. The defendants were originally indicted on fifty-eight counts for violating Section 211 of the Federal Farm Loan Act. Conviction under Section 211 carried a possible sentence of five years. Instead, the defendants were convicted of conspiracy under Section 37 of the federal code, and the maximum sentence for conspiracy was no more than two years, a fine or both. According to the indictment, Richard, Horne and Harvey "made false statements to the Federal Intermediate Credit Bank for the purpose of obtaining advances, know[ing] them to be false." Edgar A. Brown, attorney for the defense, submitted several petitions, including one for bail. The judge set bail for Richardson and Horne at $10,000 and bail for Beulah Harvey at $1,000. Upon posting bond, the defendants were released pending the outcome of their appeal. Both Richardson and Harvey were members of the Baptist Church of Beaufort.

A RIDGELAND JURY WEIGHS IN

Richardson also received more bad news in late February 1928. A jury in Ridgeland, Jasper County, found Richardson and W.P. Jay guilty of making "false statements." Richardson was president and Jay cashier of the former Beaufort Bank. Originally, Richardson, Jay and R.C. Horne had been charged with "conspiracy in lending to the American Ship Building Company." The indictment against Jay was dropped and the case against Richardson and Horne prosecuted. Among the witnesses for the prosecution were Edward Nelson, E.O. Wilson and O.H. Davis, who had served as the bank's assistant cashier. The jury only needed thirty minutes to reach a verdict. Judge M.L. Bonham sentenced the men to twelve months in the state penitentiary or on "the public works of Beaufort County or a fine of five hundred dollars." Representing the defendants in this trial were Edgar A. Brown of Barnwell (later an influential state senator) and J. Heyward Jenkins of Beaufort. Representing the state were Randolph Murdaugh, George Warren, solicitor, and George Buist. Attorneys for the convicted men promised to appeal the verdict.

In their appeal, lawyers for the defense argued in the South Carolina Supreme Court case of *State v. Richardson et al.*, 149 S.C. 121, 146 S.E. 676 (1928), that Judge Bonham had erred in dismissing their motion to quash the indictment on the grounds that the members of the grand jury had been improperly drawn. The defense contended that as the board of jury commissioners for Beaufort County were "personally and officially" depositors who had lost money when the bank closed, it was improper for them to draw the names of the grand jury. At that time, the jury commissioners were J.C. Black, auditor; E.B. Rogers, clerk of court; and Gus Sanders, treasurer. The South Carolina Supreme Court upheld Bonham's ruling as the defendants, by applying to Judge De Vore for a change of venue because they could not receive a "fair and impartial trial" in Beaufort County, had "recognized the fact…that a true bill, a valid bill was returned."

In July 1928, William J. Thomas, receiver for the former Beaufort Bank, announced good news. Thanks to his research and effort, the United States government refunded $5,661,770 in overpaid taxes.

After the conviction, the Baptist Church of Beaufort, according to Annette Milliken Maddox, convened a specially called church conference on March 11, 1928. At that meeting, a majority of the congregation present voted to exclude Richardson and Harvey from church membership. Richardson had been assistant superintendent of the Sunday school. Although Richardson eventually returned to Beaufort in 1930, he and his family lived in Columbia, South Carolina, where he worked as a bookkeeper for a grocery company.

Untangling the affairs of the failed Beaufort Bank required years of effort. The courts heard related cases into the 1930s. Among those cases

A view of the Baptist Church of Beaufort as originally built without the belfry or steeple. Center of the July 1926 bank failure, Walter E. Richardson, president of the Beaufort Bank, was at one time a member of the Baptist Church of Beaufort. *Courtesy of the Library of Congress, HABS SC,7-BEAU,3-7.*

were *Federal Intermediate Credit Bank of Columbia, S.C. v. Mitchell,* Circuit Court of Appeals, Fourth Circuit, 46 F. 2d 301 (1931) and *Mitchell v. Federal Intermediate Credit Bank of Columbia, Supreme Court of South Carolina,* 165 S.C. 457, 164 S.E. 136 (1932). The legal trail ended in dashed hopes, alleged tales of mortgages secured by railroad rights of way and unemployed New Jersey residents filing applications for mortgages on Beaufort County land, ruined careers and unanswered questions. Yet in the end, many in Beaufort suffered economic hardship, and the timing of the failure only a few years before the stock market collapse on Black Thursday, October 24, 1929, presaged difficult times nationwide for the banking industry and its investors. The failure of the Beaufort Bank possibly made Beaufort residents and businesses more vulnerable to the economic depression of the 1930s. It certainly made them more leery and less trustful. The scandalous failure of the Beaufort Bank on July 10, 1926, cast a very long shadow.

EPILOGUE
And the Beat Goes On

M enace can lie in a stranger's footfall, the rustle of leaves on a lonely path, a prophet's voice, a turn of a card, unsecured credit or an ill-spoken word. Violence knows no boundaries. Mayhem lurks where the unsuspecting gather. Murder haunts history. Men live, strive and die as pawns in a global game of chess. Beaufort's first 350 or so years were ones of great striving, difficult choices, justice dispensed and justice denied.

Personal foibles, inhumanity and evil know no season, follow no calendar. As Shakespeare noted in the *Tempest*, "what's past is prologue." The sins of the past color and inform the future. Such errors of omission and commission will continue to cloud human life as long as man walks the earth. So, too, in Beaufort, menace, murder and mayhem continue to thrive beneath the live oak canopy.

Lonely vista, Beaufort County. *John R. Todd and Francis Marion Hutson,* Old Prince William's Parish and Plantations *(Richmond: Garrett & Massie, 1935).*

Bibliography

Adams, Lark Emerson, ed. *Journals of the South Carolina House of Representatives, 1785–1786*. Columbia: University of South Carolina Press for the South Carolina Department of Archives and History, 1979.

Beaufort Gazette (Beaufort, South Carolina).

Edgar, Walter. *South Carolina: A History*. Columbia: University of South Carolina Press, 1998.

Edward, Adele Stanton, ed. *Journals of the Privy Council, 1783–1789*. Columbia: University of South Carolina Press for the South Carolina Department of Archives and History, 1971.

Helsley, Alexia Jones. *Beaufort, South Carolina: A History*. Charleston, SC: The History Press, 2005.

———. *Guide to Historic Beaufort, South Carolina*. Charleston, SC: The History Press, 2006.

Heyward, Barnwell Rhett. "The Descendants of Col. William Rhett, of South Carolina." *South Carolina Historical Magazine* 4 (1903): 36–74.

Ivers, Larry E. "Scouting the Inland Passage, 1685–1737." *South Carolina Historical Magazine* 73 (1972): 117–29.

Jones, Katherine. *Port Royal under Six Flags.* Indianapolis, IN: Bobbs-Merrill Company, Inc., 1960.

Maddox, Annette Milliken. *A Lamp unto the Lowcountry: The Baptist Church of Beaufort, 1804–2004, Beaufort, South Carolina. N.p.:* Baptist History and Heritage Society and Fields Publishing, Inc., 2004.

New York Times (New York City, New York).

Reports of the State Bank Examiner Showing the Condition of South Carolina State Banks. 1909–12.

Rowland, Lawrence S. "Beaufort" and "Beaufort County." In *The South Carolina Encyclopedia,* edited by Walter Edgar. Columbia: University of South Carolina Press, 2006.

———. *Window on the Atlantic: The Rise and Fall of Santa Elena, South Carolina's Spanish City.* N.p.: South Carolina Department of Archives and History, 1990.

Rowland, Lawrence S., et al. *History of Beaufort County, South Carolina, vol. I. 1514–1861.* Columbia: University of South Carolina Press, 1996.

Salley, A.S. ed. *Minutes of the Vestry of St. Helena's Parish, South Carolina, 1726–1812.* N.p.: Historical Commission of South Carolina, 1919.

Smith, Henry A.M. "Purrysburgh." *South Carolina Historical Magazine* 10 (1909): 187–219.

South Carolina Highway Historical Marker Guide. N.p.: South Carolina Department of Archives and History, 1998. 2d. rev. ed.

South, Stanley. *Archaeology at Santa Elena: Doorway to the Past.* N.p.: South Carolina Institute of Archaeology and Anthropology, 1991.

The State (Columbia, South Carolina).

Statutes at Large of South Carolina. V, 671–72.

Stoney, Samuel Gaillard. "The Autobiography of William John Grayson." *South Carolina Historical Magazine* 49 (1948): 23–40.

Index

About the Author

A lexia Jones Helsley is a historian who loves to write about her hometown. A *magna cum laude* graduate of Furman University, she holds a master's degree from the University of South Carolina and is a member of the Beaufort High School Hall of Fame. Currently, she is an instructor in history at the University of South Carolina–Aiken and a member of the Old Exchange Commission. Among her other History Press titles are *Beaufort: A History*, *A Guide to Historic Beaufort*, *Lost Columbia: Bygone Images of South Carolina's Capital City* and *Lost Greenville County, South Carolina*. Recipient of several awards, including the Governor's Archives Award and the SCDAR Bobby Gilmer Moss Award, Helsley and her husband live near Irmo, South Carolina.

Visit us at
www.historypress.net